When We Are Married

A Yorkshire Farcical Comedy

J. B. Priestley

Samuel French - London
New York - Toronto - Hollywood

D1288524

© 1938 BY J. B. PRIESTLEY
© (IN RENEWAL) 1966 BY J. B. PRIESTLEY

Rights of Performance by Amateurs are controlled by Samuel French Ltd, 52 Fitzroy Street, London W1P 6JR, and they, or their authorized agents, issue licences to amateurs on payment of a fee. **It is an infringement of the Copyright to give any performance or public reading of the play before the fee has been paid and the licence issued.**

The Royalty Fee indicated below is subject to contract and subject to variation at the sole discretion of Samuel French Ltd.

Basic fee for each and every
performance by amateurs   Code M
in the British Isles

The publication of this play does not imply that it is necessarily available for performance by amateurs or professionals, either in the British Isles or Overseas. Amateurs and professionals considering a production are strongly advised in their own interests to apply to the appropriate agents for consent before starting rehearsals or booking a theatre or hall.

ISBN 0 573 01476 0

Please see page iv for further copyright information.

WHEN WE ARE MARRIED

First performed at the St. Martin's Theatre, London, on October 11th, 1938, with the following cast :

(In the order of appearance)

RUBY BIRTLE	Patricia Hayes.
GERALD FORBES	Richard Warner.
MRS. NORTHROP	Beatrice Varley.
NANCY HOLMES	Betty Fleetwood.
FRED DYSON	Alexander Grandison.
HENRY ORMONROYD	Frank Pettingell.
ALDERMAN JOSEPH HELLIWELL	Lloyd Pearson.
MARIA HELLIWELL	Muriel George.
COUNCILLOR ALBERT PARKER	Raymond Huntley.
HERBERT SOPPITT	Ernest Butcher.
CLARA SOPPITT	Ethel Coleridge.
ANNIE PARKER	Helena Pickard.
LOTTIE GRADY	Mai Bacon.
REV. CLEMENT MERCER	Norman Wooland.
MAYOR OF CLECKLEWYKE	H. Marsh Dunn.

A BASIL DEAN Production.

The action takes place in the sitting-room of Alderman Helliwell's house in Clecklewyke, a town in the West Riding, on an evening about thirty years ago.

ACT I

A September evening.

ACT II

About half an hour later.

ACT III

About a quarter of an hour later.

COPYRIGHT INFORMATION

(See also page ii)

This play is fully protected under the Copyright Laws of the British Common-wealth of Nations, the United States of America and all countries of the Berne and Universal Copyright Conventions.

All rights, including Stage, Motion Picture, Radio, Television, Public Reading, and Translation into Foreign Languages are strictly reserved.

No part of this publication may lawfully be reproduced in ANY form or by any means — photocopying, typescript, recording (including video-recording), manuscript, electronic, mechanical, or otherwise — or be transmitted or stored in a retrieval system, without prior permission.

Licences for amateur performances are issued subject to the understanding that it shall be made clear in all advertising matter that the audience will witness an amateur performance; that the names of the authors of the plays shall be included on all announcements and on all programmes; and that the integrity of the authors' work will be preserved.

The Royalty Fee is subject to contract and subject to variation at the sole discretion of Samuel French Ltd.

In Theatres or Halls seating Four Hundred or more the fee will be subject to negotiation.

In Territories Overseas the fee quoted in this Acting Edition may not apply. A fee will be quoted on application to our local authorized agent, or if there is no such agent, on application to Samuel French Ltd, London.

VIDEO RECORDING OF AMATEUR PRODUCTIONS

Please note that the copyright laws governing video-recording are extremely complex and that it should not be assumed that any play may be video-recorded *for whatever purpose* without first obtaining the permission of the appropriate agents. The fact that a play is published by Samuel French Ltd does not indicate that video rights are available or that Samuel French Ltd controls such rights.

WHEN WE ARE MARRIED*

ACT I

SCENE.—*The sitting-room in Helliwell's house.*
It is a solid detached late-Victorian house. On the L. (*actor's* L.)
wall is a window. L.C. *in the back wall is a door to the rest of
the house, leading directly into the hall. On the* R. *wall is a small
conservatory, with a door leading into this, and then into the
garden. The room is furnished without taste, in the style of about
thirty years ago. There is an upright piano, little cupboards,
drawers in small tables, etc.*

At the rise of the CURTAIN, *the evening sunlight comes through the
window. There is nobody on the stage. We hear the front-
door bell ring. A moment later,* RUBY BIRTLE *ushers in* GERALD
FORBES. RUBY *is a very young " slavey " of the period, who
looks as if her hair has just gone " up."* FORBES *is a pleasant
young man, in the smart clothes of the period, and unlike* RUBY
*and most of the other characters does not talk with a marked
West Riding accent.*

RUBY (L. *of the door*). You'll have to wait, 'cos they haven't
finished their tea.

GERALD. Bit late, aren't they ? (*He crosses to* R.C.)

RUBY (*approaching, confidentially*). It's a do.

GERALD. It's what ?

RUBY. A do. Y'know, they've company.

GERALD. Oh—I see. It's a sort of party, and they're having
high tea.

RUBY (*after nodding, going closer still*). Roast pork, stand pie,
salmon and salad, trifle, two kinds o' jellies, lemon-cheese tarts,
jam tarts, swiss tarts, sponge cake, walnut cake, chocolate roll,
and a pound cake kept from last Christmas.

GERALD (*with irony*). Is that all ?

RUBY (*seriously*). No, there's white bread, brown bread,
currant teacake, one o' them big curd tarts from Gregory's, and
a lot o' cheese.

GERALD. It *is* a do, isn't it ? (*He moves towards the conservatory.*)

RUBY (*after nodding, then very confidentially*). *And* a little
brown jug.

GERALD (*turning, astonished*). A little brown jug ?

RUBY (*still confidentially*). You know what that is, don't you ? *Don't* you ? (*She laughs.*) Well, I never did ! Little brown jug's a drop o' rum for your tea. They're getting right lively on it. (*Coolly.*) But you don't come from round here, do you ?

GERALD (*down R., not disposed for a chat*). No.

(*A distant bell rings, not the front-door bell.*)

RUBY. I come from near Rotherham. Me father works in t'pit, and so does our Frank and our Wilfred.

(*The distant bell sounds again.*)

GERALD. There's a bell ringing somewhere.

RUBY (*coolly*). I know. It's for me. Let her wait. She's run me off me legs to-day. And Mrs. Northrop's in t'kitchen—she can do a bit for a change. (*She crosses to* GERALD.) There's seven of 'em at it in t'dining-room—Alderman Helliwell and missus, of course—then Councillor Albert Parker and Mrs. Parker, and Mr. Herbert Soppitt and Mrs. Soppitt—and of course Miss Holmes.

GERALD. Oh—Miss Holmes *is* there, is she ?

RUBY. Yes, but she's stopped eating. (*She giggles.*) You're courting her, aren't you ?

GERALD (*astonished and alarmed*). What !

RUBY (*coolly*). Oh—I saw you both—the other night, near Cleckley Woods. I was out meself, with our milkman's lad.

(GERALD *turns away.*)

Now don't look like that, I won't tell on you.

GERALD (*producing a shilling, then rather desperately*). Now—look here ! What's your name ?

RUBY. Ruby Birtle.

GERALD. Well, Ruby, you wouldn't like Miss Holmes to get into a row here with her uncle and aunt, would you ?

RUBY. No, I wouldn't like that. But I'd like that shilling.

GERALD (*after giving it to her*). You said Miss Holmes had finished eating.

RUBY. Yes. She can't put it away like some of 'em. I'd rather keep Councillor Albert Parker a week than a fortnight. D'you want to see her ?

GERALD. Yes. Could you just give her the tip quietly that I'm here—if the rest of them aren't coming in here yet ?

RUBY. Not them ! You'd think they'd been pined for a month—way they're going at it ! (*She turns up stage.*) I'll tell her. (*She turns back.*) She'd better come round that way—through t'greenhouse——

(*Before she can move again,* MRS. NORTHROP, *an aggressive but humorous working-woman of about fifty, puts her head in through the doorway.*)

MRS. NORTHROP (*aggressively*). Oh—'ere y'are !

RUBY (*coolly*). That's right, Mrs. Northrop. (*She crosses up* L.C.)

MRS. NORTHROP (*aggressively*). I see nought right about it— you gassin' in 'ere as if you owned t'place instead o' gettin' on wi' your work. She's rung for yer twice, an' I've just taken another lot o' hot water in. Nah, come on, yer little crackpot ι

(*She holds the door open, and* RUBY *exits after a grin at* GERALD. MRS. NORTHROP *looks in for a minute.*)

Aren't you t'organist at chapel ? (*She moves down a little.*)

GERALD. Yes.

MRS. NORTHROP (*cheerfully*). Ay, well, they've got it in for you.

GERALD (*astonished*). How do you know ?

MRS. NORTHROP. 'Cos I 'eard 'em say so. (*Complacently.*) I don't miss much.

GERALD (*slowly*). So that's why Mr. Helliwell asked me to come round and see him.

MRS. NORTHROP (*cheerfully*). That's right. There's three of 'em 'ere to-night, d'you see—all big men at chapel. You've been enjoyin' yerself a bit too much, I fancy, lad.

GERALD (*slowly*). So that's it—is it ?

MRS. NORTHROP (*coming a little farther in, leaning forward, with a very confidential air*). Ay—and d'you know what I say ? I say—to 'ell with 'em !

(*She turns up and exits, leaving* GERALD *looking a little worried. He moves about restlessly towards* L., *takes his cigarette-case out of his pocket mechanically, then puts it back again. He keeps an eye on the door into the conservatory. After a few moments,* NANCY HOLMES, *an attractive girl in her early twenties, hurries in through this doorway, and checks down* R.)

NANCY (*in breathless whisper*). Gerald !

GERALD (*joyfully advancing*). Nancy ! (*He makes as if to kiss her.*)

NANCY (*breathlessly*). No, you mustn't, not here—no, Gerald —please——

(*But he does kiss her and no harm has been done. They sit on the* R. *settee,* GERALD *on her* R.)

Now, listen, Gerald, and be sensible. This is serious. You know why Uncle Joe sent for you ?

GERALD (*with a slight grin*). They've *got it in for* me. I've just been told.

NANCY. It's serious, Gerald. They've been grumbling about you some time, and now, as far as I .can gather, one of these miserable old beasts saw you late one night—with *me*——

GERALD (*serious now*). Oh—I say—you weren't recognized, were you ?

NANCY. No. But *you* were.

GERALD. Well, that's not so bad, as long as they can't drag you into it. I know how strict your aunt is, and you can't afford to quarrel with them here until we're ready to be married——

NANCY (*earnestly*). No, but you can't either, Gerald. And they're going to be very cross with you, and you'll have to be awfully careful what you say to them. And there's that beastly Councillor Parker here, too, and you loathe him, don't you ?

GERALD. Absolutely. And I'll loathe him more than ever now that he's full of roast pork and trifle. (*He rises, moving to above the* L. *settee.*) I think I'd better give them time to recover from that huge ghastly tuck-in they're having.

NANCY. I should. Though they've nearly finished now.

GERALD (*returns to the* R. *settee*). If I clear out for half an hour or so, could you slip away too ? (*He sits.*)

NANCY. I might. They don't really want me. I'm in the way. You see, it's an anniversary celebration, and I don't come into it at all.

GERALD. What are they celebrating ?

(*Before she can reply,* RUBY *opens the door, announcing.*)

RUBY. It's " Yorkshire Argus "—two of 'em.

(GERALD *rises, and moves down* R.
     Enter FRED DYSON, *a cheerful, rather cheeky youngish reporter, and* HENRY ORMONROYD, *who carries a large and old-fashioned newspaperman's camera and a flashlight apparatus.* ORMON-ROYD *is a middle-aged man with an air of beery dignity and wears a large drooping moustache.* NANCY *has risen. She crosses up* L.C.)

This is Miss Holmes, Alderman Helliwell's niece. T'others is still having their tea.

(RUBY *goes out.* DYSON *comes down to* NANCY.)

DYSON (*cheerfully*). 'Evening, Miss Holmes. (*To* GERALD.) How-d'you-do ? This is Mr. Henry Ormonroyd, our photo-grapher. (*He crosses down* L.)

ORMONROYD (*bowing*). Pleased to meet you, I'm sure. Delightful weather we're having for the time of year.

GERALD. Isn't it ?

ORMONROYD (*profoundly*). It is.

DYSON. We seem to have come too early.

NANCY. I'm afraid you have——

ORMONROYD (*with dignified reproach*). What did I tell you, Fred ? (*He moves to* DYSON.) Always wanting to rush things. We could have had at least a couple more with my friend at the " Lion." (*He crosses to* C.) He's a chap who used to have a very good little peppermint rock business on the Central Pier, Blackpool, at the time I had my studio there. Old times, y'know, Mr. —er—and happy days, happy days ! (*He turns up stage, humming.*)

DYSON (*briskly, moving to* L.C.). All right, Henry. I'm sorry we're early. Matter of fact, I don't know yet what this is about. I just got a message from the office to come up here and bring a photographer.

NANCY. You see, it's their Silver Wedding.

DYSON. Henry ! It's Alderman Helliwell's *Silver Wedding* !

ORMONROYD. Very nice—I suppose.

NANCY. Yes, but not only my uncle and aunt's. There were three couples—my uncle and aunt, Mr. and Mrs. Soppitt, Mr. and Mrs. Parker——

DYSON. Is that Councillor Albert Parker ?

NANCY (*pulling a little face*). Yes. You know him ?

DYSON (*gloomily*). Yes, we know him.

ORMONROYD (*confidentially*). Every time he opens his mouth at the Town Hall, he puts his foot in it, so they call him the " foot and mouth disease "—— Ha ! ha ! (*Now suddenly solemn again.*) Are all three happy couples here ?

NANCY. Yes, because they were all married on the same morning at the same chapel. They have a photograph—a combined wedding-group. (*She goes to the piano to find it.*)

GERALD (*to* DYSON, *moving in to* R.C.). You'll have to interview 'em, and they'll tell you how happy they've been—— (*He sits on the* R. *settee.*)

DYSON. Oh—yes. I see the idea now.

NANCY (*returning with an old photograph*). Here you are. All six of them on their wedding morning. Don't they look absurd in those clothes ?

ORMONROYD (*solemnly*). To you—yes. To me—no. I was married myself about that time. (*Holding the photograph at arm's length, and looking at it critically.*) Now, you see, Fred (*he crosses down to* DYSON), what's wanted is another group in the very same positions—— After twenty-five years' wear and tear. Very nice.

DYSON. You're holding it upside down.

ORMONROYD. I know, lad, I know. That's the way we always look at 'em professionally. (*He looks closely.*) Either the flies have been at this, or someone's touched up Albert Parker with a screw-driver. (*He gives the photograph to* GERALD.) Well, if

we're too early, we're too early. Might nip back to the " Lion,"
Fred lad, eh ?

(ORMONROYD *takes the camera from the top of the settee* L.)

DYSON. We'll come back in about an hour.

ORMONROYD. They're keeping a very nice drop of beer down
at the " Lion," now.

(DYSON *and* ORMONROYD *go out,* NANCY *going towards the door
with them, and shutting it behind them.* GERALD *looks at the
photograph, then at the back of it, and is obviously interested and
amused.*)

GERALD (*moving to* C., *with some excitement*). This was when
they were all married, then—September the fifth, 'eighty-
three ?

NANCY. Yes—why ? (*Coming down* C.) What's the matter,
Gerald ? (*He has started laughing.*) Gerald, what is it ? Oh—
don't be so mean. They'll be here in a minute.

(*As he shakes his head, still laughing softly, we hear voices behind
the door into the hall.*)

GERALD. They're coming in. Nancy, let's dodge out that
way.

(*He puts down the photograph on the table below the* R. *settee, picks up
his straw hat, while she has gone to the door into the conservatory, and
they hurry out that way, shutting the door behind them. Voices
outside the door into the hall are louder now, and after a moment
the* PARKERS, *the* SOPPITTS *and the* HELLIWELLS *enter. They
are dressed in their best, and obviously crammed with high tea.*
ALBERT PARKER *is a tall, thin, conceited, sententious man ; his
wife* ANNIE, *a hopeful kind of woman.* HERBERT SOPPITT *is a
smallish, neat man, clearly dominated by his wife* CLARA, *a noisy
woman.* JOSEPH *and* MARIA HELLIWELL *are high-coloured,
rather bouncing, rather pompous, very pleased with themselves
Their ages are all between forty-five and fifty-five.* HERBERT
SOPPITT *and* MRS. PARKER *talk a rather genteel ordinary Eng-
lish ; the other four have pronounced North-Country accents,
with particularly broad " a " sounds.*)

HELLIWELL (*very much the host*). Now what's wanted now's
a good cigar, an' I've got the very thing. (*He goes to get a box
from the drawer of the table.*)

(PARKER *and* SOPPITT *move to* R.C., *above the settee.*)

MARIA (*indignantly*). That Mrs. Northrop ! When she's
finished her washing-up to-night she goes—and goes for good.

CLARA. And quite right too ! They're all the same. Answering back—if you say anything.

MARIA. Trouble with her is—she likes a drop. I've smelt it before to-day.

(CLARA *sits on the lower end of the settee* L.C., MARIA *at the upper end.* ANNIE *crosses, and sits below the settee* R.C.)

HELLIWELL (C., *offering the cigar-box to* PARKER). Now then, Albert ! You'll find that's a good cigar, La Corona.

PARKER (*taking one*). Thanks, Joe. As you know, I don't smoke a lot, but when I do, I like a good cigar.

HELLIWELL (*offering to* SOPPITT). Herbert ?

SOPPITT. I don't think—er—I will—thanks, Joe.

MARIA (*expansively*). Nay, Herbert, 'ave one o' Joe's cigars.

CLARA. If he'd had it to pay for himself, he'd have been wanting one.

SOPPITT (*rather nervously*). I think—I'd rather not smoke just now—I believe I ate too much at tea.

ANNIE (*to keep him company*). I know *I* did.

(SOPPITT *moves to the conservatory.*)

PARKER (*severely*). Yes, an' you'll be complaining before the night's out. (*He comes to the settee* R.C. *and sits on* ANNIE'S L.)

CLARA. An' so will Herbert.

PARKER (*complacently*). Now that's something that never bothers me.

HELLIWELL (C., *guffawing*). No, we've noticed that, Albert.

PARKER (*offended*). How d'you mean ?

MARIA. Go on, Albert, you know what Joe is—must 'ave his little joke.

ANNIE. I know *I* ought to have stopped long before I did—I mean, at tea—but, Maria, everything was *so* nice.

CLARA. 'Ear, 'ear !

MARIA (*complacently accepting this*). Well, I said to Joe, " Now, Joe," I said, " we'll only have just the six of us, but we'll make it an occasion an' do it well while we're at it," I said. Didn't I, Joe ?

HELLIWELL (*busy attending to his cigar, though he does not remove the band*). Did you ?

MARIA (*indignantly*). You know very well I did.

HELLIWELL (*still not interested*). All right, you did then.

MARIA (*same indignant tone*). You know quite well I did, Joe Helliwell.

HELLIWELL (*suddenly annoyed himself*). All right, all right, all right, you did then.

CLARA (*pats* MARIA'S *hands*). They're all alike. Wait till somebody else's with you, and then try to make you out a liar.

PARKER (*severely*). Speak for yourself ! I don't try to make my wife out a liar. do I, Annie ?

ANNIE (*rather timidly, hesitantly*). Well—no—Albert, not—really——

PARKER (*very severely*). How d'you mean—*not really*—I just don't, that's all. (*Changing the subject, in rather lordly style.*) A good smoke, Joe, quite a good smoke. It reminds me of that cigar Sir Harold Watson gave me not so long since at the club. I was standing near the fireplace, and Sir Harold came up——

ANNIE (*gathering courage to interrupt*). Albert—you told them before.

PARKER (*glaring*). Well, I can tell 'em again, can't I ?

SOPPITT (*tactfully, coming to below the* R. *settee*). Maria, have you got a copy of that old photograph we had taken ? I couldn't find ours.

MARIA. Yes. Where is it, Joe ? (*While he looks round.*) Aaa, I laugh many a time when I think o' that morning—six of us, all so nervous——

HELLIWELL. And the parson worse still. He was only like twopennorth o' copper, an' I could ha' given him a few years myself.

CLARA. I think we were about first he'd ever married.

ANNIE. I'm sure we were. I didn't feel I'd been married properly——

PARKER (*severely*). Of course you'd been married properly. If he'd been ninety and doing it all his life, you wouldn't ha' been married any better, would you ?

MARIA. I've forgotten his name now. He was only a temporary, wasn't he ?

SOPPITT. I remember ! (*A pause.*) It was a tree—Beech.

HELLIWELL. That's right—Beech—an' he'd a funny squint. (*He has found the photograph.*) And here's the old photo. (*He hands it to his wife.* ANNIE *crosses to the* L. *settee, and the ladies look at it, with exclamations, while the men remain aloof.*)

PARKER (*the business-man now*). I see Crossbreds are down again.

HELLIWELL (*another business-man*). Ay—and they'll stay down with Australian market as it is. (*He sits in the chair* C.) If I've said it once, I've said it a thousand times—if Merinos is down and staying down, then your Crossbreds'll have to follow. Now, look at Merinos——

MARIA (*looking up to expostulate*). Here, Joe, we didn't come here to talk about Merinos. This isn't Wool Exchange. Take a look at yourselves and see what we took on.

(*He ignores her. She puts the photograph on the table behind the settee.*)

HELLIWELL. Now wait a minute. 'Ealths !

MARIA. That's right, Joe. Ring !

(HELLIWELL *rings.* MARIA *turns to the others.*)

We ought to do it in proper style, an' drink our healths before
we go any further.

SOPPITT (*attempting a joke*). Further—where ?

CLARA (*severely*). That'll do, Herbert. A bit o' fun's all right,
but you go too far.

SOPPITT (*indignantly*). I didn't mean——

CLARA (*rises, cutting in*). That'll do, Herbert ! (*She crosses
to the settee R., and sits.*)

(MRS. NORTHROP *looks in.*)

MRS. NORTHROP (*aggressively*). Well ?

MARIA (*rather grandly*). There's a tray with glasses on—just
bring it in——

MRS. NORTHROP (*indignantly*). What—me ? How many
pairs of 'ands——

HELLIWELL (*peremptorily*). *Now then*—just tell thingumpty-
ite—Ruby—to bring in the port wine.

MRS. NORTHROP. What—on top o' your tea ? You'll be
poorly.

(*She withdraws.* HELLIWELL *is furious.*)

HELLIWELL (*angrily*). Now did you 'ear that——

MARIA (*hastily*). All right, Joe, we don't want any trouble.
She goes to-night, an' she doesn't come back.

CLARA. I don't know what things are coming to ! All the
same ! Answering back !

PARKER (*sententiously*). They're all alike, that class of people.
We have the same trouble at mill. Don't know when they're
well off. Idle, that's what they are—bone idle !

CLARA. *And* impudent ! Back answers !

ANNIE (*timidly*). Yes—but I suppose they don't know any
better——

PARKER (*severely*). They know a lot better. And what you
want to stick up for 'em for, I can't think.

HELLIWELL (*heartily*). Now then, Albert, don't start fratch-
ing, but try an' enjoy yourself for once. This is an anniversary.
Which reminds me, Charlie Pearson told me, t'other day, they
built a new Wesleyan Methodist Chapel up at Thornton, and they
opened with an anniversary. Anyhow, this is ours, so let's have
peace an' goodwill all round. Now I thought we'd first drink
a bit of a toast to ourselves——

MARIA. That was *my* idea.

HELLIWELL (*ignoring this, but only just*). Then I thought we'd
have a bit of a chat about old times, an' then we'd settle down to
a game o' Newmarket——

MARIA. That was my idea too.

HELLIWELL (*annoyed*). What the hangment does it matter
whose idea it was, so long as we get on with it and enjoy ourselves !

SOPPITT. That's the great thing. (*Controlled belch. He catches his wife's eye and falters.*) Enjoy ourselves. (*He rises, moves to the R. door, looking miserable and a bit sick.*)

CLARA (*severely*). I told you to leave that salmon alone.

HELLIWELL (*moves down a step*). Nay, Clara, why can't he have a bit o' salmon if he fancies it ?

CLARA (*sharply*). 'Cos it doesn't fancy him, Joe Helliwell, that's why. Look at that time we all went to Scarborough !

SOPPITT. It was Bridlington. (*She turns back to the R. end of the settee.*)

CLARA. It was both ! And what did that doctor say ? *You're digging your grave with your teeth, Mr. Soppitt.*

HELLIWELL. Ha-ha-ha !

(*Enter RUBY, carrying a tray with six small glasses on it, and three bottles of port. HELLIWELL crosses up to her.*)

Here, what did you want to bring 'em all for ? One bottle at a time's enough.

RUBY (*putting down the tray*). Mrs. Northrop said you'd better 'ave t'lot while you was at it.

HELLIWELL (*heavily*). In future, just take your orders from me and not from Mrs. Northrop. Now just trot along—an' no lip.

(*He starts to take the cork out of the bottle.*)

RUBY (*turning at the door*). Mrs. Northrop says she's not coming 'ere again——

HELLIWELL (*heatedly*). We know all about it. (*He moves after her, cigar in mouth, bottle in hand.*)

MARIA (*cutting in*). Now let it be, Joe.

(HELLIWELL *draws the cork with an effort.*)

(RUBY *has now gone and closed the door.* HELLIWELL *begins pouring out the port.*)

D'you know what we ought to do for this ? We ought to get just in the same places we were in that old photo. Where is it ? (*She finds it and directs them from it.*) Now here we are. (*She uses a settee.*) I was in the middle. You were here, Clara. You this side, Annie. Now come on, Albert—behind Annie. Herbert.

(MARIA *sits last. These five have now arranged themselves in the grouping of the old photograph.* HELLIWELL *hands them their glasses of port, then takes up a position himself.*)

HELLIWELL (*facetiously*). Here's to me and my wife's husband !

MARIA. Let's have none o' that silly nonsense, Joe.

PARKER (*solemnly*). A few serious words is what's needed.

ANNIE (*rather plaintively*). Oh—must you, Albert ?

PARKER. How d'you mean—must I ? What's wrong with a few serious words on an occasion like this ? Marriage—is a serious business.

CLARA. That's right, Albert. Where'd we be without it ?

SOPPITT. Single.

CLARA. That'll do, Herbert.

PARKER (*sententiously, moving to* C., *facing the others*). Marriage —well—marriage—to begin with, it's an institution, isn't it ?

MARIA (*solemnly*). That is so. (*Sighs profoundly.*)

PARKER (*getting into his stride*). One of the *oldest* institutions. It goes back—right back to—well, it goes right back. And it's still going strong to-day. Why ?

HELLIWELL (*hastily*). Well, because——

PARKER (*sharply cutting in*). Let me finish, Joe, let me finish. Now, why is it still going strong to-day ? Because it's the backbone of a decent respectable life.

HELLIWELL (*solemnly*). True, Albert, true.

PARKER. Where would women be without marriage ?

CLARA (*sharply*). And where'd some o' you men be ?

PARKER. All right, I'm coming to that.

HELLIWELL. Well, don't be too long, Albert. I want to try this port.

PARKER (*solemnly*). Marriage may be a bit more necessary to women than it is to men——

ANNIE. Why ?

PARKER (*annoyed at this*). *Why ?*

HELLIWELL. Children, you see, Annie.

ANNIE (*abashed*). Oh—yes—I'd forgotten. Still——

PARKER. I'm talking now, *if* you please. But if a woman wants a 'ome and security and a respectable life, *which* she gets from marriage, a man wants something to——

CLARA (*quickly*). He wants all he can get.

PARKER. He wants a nice comfortable 'ome, somebody to tell his troubles to and so forth——

HELLIWELL (*facetiously*). That's good, Albert, the *and so forth*.

PARKER. Now, Joe——

HELLIWELL. Well, cut it short——

PARKER (*slowly and solemnly, moving back to the top of the settee* R.). So, as we're all gathered 'ere to celebrate the anniversary of our joint wedding-day, friends, I give you—the toast of *Marriage* !

MARIA. Very nice, Albert.

(*They all drink.*)

ANNIE (*confidentially*). It'll go straight to my head. D'you remember that time at Harrogate ? I could have sunk through the floor when that waiter laughed.

HELLIWELL (*producing the bottle again from the table* R.C.). Now, wait a minute. That's all right as far as it goes—but—nay—damn it !——

MARIA (*reproachfully*). Joe !

HELLIWELL. We must have another toast, just for ourselves. I bet it isn't often there's three couples can meet like this who were all wed on same morning together. Now then——

(*He insists on filling the glasses again as they still hold them in their hands. He takes the bottle back to the table.*)

MARIA (*confidentially*). I don't act silly, but my face gets so red.

HELLIWELL. Now—here's to all of us—and the Reverend Mr. What's-his-name—Beech—who tied us up—wherever he is——

THE OTHERS. Here's to us. Here's to him. (*Etc.*)

(*They drink. When they have finished, the front-door bell is heard.*)

MARIA. Front door ! Who'll that be ?

HELLIWELL (*rather importantly*). Well, I told " Yorkshire Argus " to send somebody round to have a word with us.

CLARA (*delighted*). What—are you going to have a piece in the papers ?

PARKER. They don't want to catch us like this.

(*He swallows the rest of his port hastily. The others do the same. The group breaks up, PARKER to the table R.C., then down R. SOPPITT behind the table, then to the head of the settee. JOE to above the L. settee. RUBY enters.*)

MARIA. Is it " Yorkshire Argus " ?

RUBY. No, it's Mr. Forbes, t'organist from t'chapel. He came afore, an' then went away again.

HELLIWELL. Tell him to wait.

(*RUBY goes. HELLIWELL turns to the others.*)

You know about this business, Albert. You too, Herbert.

SOPPITT (*hesitantly, moving to HELLIWELL*). Yes—but——

HELLIWELL (*sharply*). But, nothing. You're too soft, Herbert.

CLARA. I'm always telling him so.

HELLIWELL. He's chapel organist—he's paid for t'job—an' either he behaves himself properly or he goes.

PARKER (*severely*). He'll go anyhow, if I've *my* say.

ANNIE. No, Albert, he's not a bad young fellow——

PARKER. Now you shut up, Annie. You don't know half of what we know. An' I'll bet we don't know half there is to know about that chap. Never should ha' been appointed. I said so then. I say so now. I know my own mind.

ANNIE (*rebelliously*). I wish sometimes you'd keep a bit of it to yourself.

PARKER. What's that mean ?

(NANCY *now appears at the door from the conservatory* R.)

MARIA. Hello, love, where've you been ?

NANCY (*who seems a trifle giggly*). Just out a minute. (*Crossing up to the door.*) You don't want me, do you, Auntie ? Because if you don't, I thought I'd put my hat and coat on and see if Muriel Spencer's in.

MARIA (*rises*). All right. (*As she moves across.*) There's that Gerald Forbes waiting outside—your uncle has something to say to him—now don't go talking to him. (*She puts the glass on the buffet, and moves to* R. *of* HELLIWELL.)

HELLIWELL. I should think not. (*Moving towards* NANCY.) Just say " Hello " or " Good evening " and leave it at that. The less you have to do with that chap the better, Nancy.

(NANCY *suddenly explodes into giggles.*)

Now what's funny about that ?

NANCY (*still giggling*). I'm sorry, Uncle. I just remembered —something that amused me——

(*She goes out giggling.*)

HELLIWELL. Now what's got hold of her ?

MARIA. Oh—she's at silly age. They don't know half the time whether to laugh or cry when they're that age. (*She goes to the top of the settee* L.C.) Now, Clara—Annie—we'll leave the men to it. I expect that's what they want——

(CLARA *comes round below the settee and up to* MARIA.)

PARKER (*solemnly*). Certainly. After all, it's chapel business.

MARIA. Well, we want to go upstairs anyhow.

HELLIWELL. That's right.

(CLARA *glares. He collapses on the settee.*)

MARIA. You haven't seen what Joe bought me yet. (*To* JOE.) But don't take too long over him.

PARKER. Him ! It wouldn't take me long——

HELLIWELL (*jovially*). It'll take me less long, 'cos I don't make speeches. Here, we'll put these out o' t'way——

(*As the women go out,* HELLIWELL *puts the glasses back on the buffet. A certain primness now descends on them.* PARKER *sits at the* L. *end of the settee* R.)

PARKER. I said from first—it's a bad appointment. To start with, he's too young.

SOPPITT (*rather timidly*). I don't think that matters much. (*He sits on* PARKER'S L.)

PARKER (*severely*). Trouble with you, Herbert, is you don't think anything matters much, and that's just where you're wrong.

HELLIWELL. Young Forbes is a southerner an' all.

PARKER (*with grim triumph*). Ah—I was coming to that.

SOPPITT. Oughtn't we to have him in ?

HELLIWELL. No, let him wait a bit.

PARKER. Do him good. No, as soon as they told me he's a Southerner and his name's Gerald, I said, " We don't want him." I said, " La-di-dah. That's what you're going to get from him," I said. " La-di-dah. What we want at Lane End—biggest chapel for miles—wi' any amount o' money in congregation—what we want is a bit o' good old Yorkshire organ-playing and choir-training," I said. " We don't want la-di-dah." (*With awful imitation of ultra-refined accents.*) " Heow-d'yew-dew. Sow chawmed to meek your acquaintance. Eoh, dee-lateful wethah ! " You know what I call that stuff ?

SOPPITT (*who has a sense of humour*). Yes. (*Broadly.*) La-di-dah.

HELLIWELL. Albert's right. We made a mistake. Mind you, he'd good qualifications, an' he seemed a nice quiet lad. But I must say, after old Sam Fawcett, chapel didn't seem right with an organist who goes round wearing one o' these pink shirts and knitted ties and creases in his trousers——

PARKER. It's all——

PARKER }
SOPPITT } (*together*). La-di-dah !

PARKER (*in a disgusted tone*). Then look at his *Messiah* ! We warned him. I said to him myself, " I know it's a Christmas piece, but you've got to get in quick, afore the others."

HELLIWELL. Right, Albert. After t'end o' November, there's been so many of 'em you might as well take your Messiah an' throw it into t'canal.

PARKER. And look what happened. Hillroad Baptist gave *Messiah*. Salem gave *Messiah*. Tong Congregational gave *Messiah*. Picklebrook Wesleyans gave *Messiah*. And where was Lane End ?

SOPPITT. Well, when we did get it—it was a good one.

HELLIWELL. I'm not saying it wasn't, but by that time who cared ? But anyhow all that's a detail. Point is, we can't have any carrying on, can we ?

SOPPITT (*gravely*). Ah—there I agree, Joe.

PARKER (*indignantly*). An' I should think so. Organist at Lane End Chapel *carrying on* ! (*He puts out his cigar, on the table behind the settee.*) That sort o' game may do down South, but it won't do up 'ere.

HELLIWELL. We're all agreed on that.

(SOPPITT *and* PARKER *nod.*)

Right, then! We'll have 'im in.

(*He goes to the door, the other two sitting up stiffly and looking official and important. Rather grimly through the open door.*)

All right, come in.

(HELLIWELL *returns to his chair* c. GERALD FORBES *follows him in, closing but not latching the door behind him.* GERALD *looks cool and self-possessed, with a twinkle in his eye.* HELLIWELL *sits down and looks as official and important as the other two. All three stare severely at* GERALD, *as he sits down.* GERALD *pulls out a cigarette-case, but no sooner has he taken a cigarette from it than* PARKER *remonstrates with him.*)

PARKER (*severely*). I wouldn't do that.

GERALD (*rather startled*). Do what?

PARKER (*severely*). Well, what 'ave you got in your 'and?

GERALD (*still surprised*). This? Cigarette. Why?

PARKER. Under the circumstances, young man, don't you think it might be better—more—more suitable—more fitting—if you didn't smoke that just now?

(*The three men look at one another.*)

GERALD (*with a shrug*). Oh—all right, if that's how you feel about it. (*Puts the case away. A pause.*) Well? You wanted to talk about something, didn't you? (*He sits at the upper end of the settee* L.C.)

HELLIWELL (*firmly*). We did. We do.

PARKER. And if I'd 'ad *my* way, we'd have been talking to you long since.

GERALD. Well, not very long since, because I haven't been up here very long.

PARKER. No, you haven't been up here very long, and I don't think you'll be up here much longer.

HELLIWELL. Here, Albert, let *me* get a word in. Mr. Forbes, you're organist of our Lane End Chapel, and that's the biggest place o' worship round here, and this is a very respectable neighbourhood, with a lot o' money behind it. You have a paid appointment as organist and choir-master.

GERALD. Yes, though it doesn't keep me, y'know, Mr. Helliwell.

HELLIWELL. No, but because you *are* our organist, you're able to get pupils and various extra jobs, so you don't do so bad out of it, eh?

GERALD (*a trifle dubiously*). No, I'm quite satisfied—for the time being.

PARKER (*annoyed*). You're satisfied! For the time being! You're satisfied!

GERALD (*quietly*). That's what I said, Mr. Parker.

PARKER *(with dignity)*. Councillor Parker. *(Pointing.)* Alderman Helliwell. Councillor Parker. *Mr.* Soppitt.

GERALD *(indicating himself)*. Plain mud!

PARKER *(explosively, rising)*. Now listen——

HELLIWELL *(cutting in noisily)*. Nay, let me finish, Albert. We want to keep calm about this—just keep calm.

(PARKER *sits.*)

GERALD. I'm quite calm.

HELLIWELL *(rather explosively)*. You're a damn' sight too calm for my liking, young man. You ought to be sitting there looking right ashamed of yourself, instead of looking—looking—well, as you do look.

GERALD. But you haven't told me what's wrong yet.

PARKER *(angrily)*. Wrong? You're wrong. And carrying on's wrong.

HELLIWELL *(loftily)*. In some chapels they mightn't care what you did—I don't know—but Lane End's got a position to keep up. We're respectable folk, and naturally we expect our organist to *behave* respectably.

SOPPITT *(apologetically)*. I think you have been very careless, Mr. Forbes, and there really has been a lot of grumbling.

PARKER. For one thing—you've been seen out—late at night—wi' girls.

GERALD. Girls?

HELLIWELL. It may be t'same lass each time, for all I know, but if what I hear is true, whoever she is, she ought to be ashamed of herself. My word, if she'd owt to do wi' me, I'd teach her a sharp lesson.

PARKER. Somebody saw you once, gallivanting away late at night, at Morecambe. And it gets round, y'know—oh yes—it gets round.

GERALD *(beginning to lose his temper)*. Yes, so it seems. But I didn't think you'd find it worth while to listen to a lot of silly gossip——

PARKER *(sharply)*. Now don't start taking that tone——

GERALD. What tone can I take? I say, a lot of silly gossip——

SOPPITT. Now, steady, steady.

GERALD. Silly gossip. Old women's twaddle——

HELLIWELL *(heavily)*. That'll do. Just remember, you're not much more than a lad yet. We're nearly twice your age, and we know what's what——

GERALD *(angrily)*. Well, what is what, then?

HELLIWELL *(angrily)*. This is what. We're not going to have any more of this. Either behave yourself, or get back to where you came from. You're not going to make us a laughing-stock and a byword in t'neighbourhood. Now this is a fair warning——

GERALD (*steadily*). I haven't done anything I'm ashamed of.

PARKER. What's that prove ? If a chap's got cheek of a brass monkey, he never need do aught he's ashamed of.

SOPPITT. Careful, Albert.

PARKER. Why should I be careful ? I'll tell him to his face what I've said behind his back. He never ought to have been appointed, and now he's been carrying on and not caring tuppence what respectable folk might think, he oughtn't to be given any warnings but told to get back to where he came from, and then he can carry on as much as he likes.

(*Both* GERALD *and* SOPPITT *start to protest, but* HELLIWELL *loudly stops them.*)

HELLIWELL. Now, Albert, we mustn't be too hard. We must give young men just another chance. (*Severely and patronizingly to* GERALD.) I'm not sure I should if this were any other time. But nay—damn it, this is a festive occasion an' we must take it easy a bit. So I'm giving you a last chance to mend yourself. And you can think yourself lucky catching me i' this humour. Just happens we're all celebrating anniversary of our wedding-day—all three of us—ay, we've all been married twenty-five years to-day. (*He blows his nose.*)

(GERALD *shakes his head rather sadly.*)

What you're shaking your head about ?

GERALD (*quietly, gently*). Well, you see, Mr. Helliwell—I beg your pardon, Alderman Helliwell—I'm rather afraid you haven't been married twenty-five years.

HELLIWELL (*roaring*). Do you think we can't count, lad ?

GERALD (*same quiet tone*). No, I don't mean that. But I'm afraid you've only been living together all this time.

HELLIWELL (*jumping up angrily*). *Living together !* I'll knock your head right off your shoulders, lad, if you start talking like that to me.

GERALD (*also standing up*). No, no, no. I'm not trying to insult you. I mean what I say.

PARKER (*angrily*). Mean what you say ! You're wrong in your damned 'ead.

SOPPITT (*authoritatively for him*). Wait a minute—Albert, Joe. We must listen. He means it.

HELLIWELL (*angrily*). Means it ! Means what ?

GERALD (*impressively*). If you'll just be quiet a minute I'll explain.

PARKER (*explosively*). I don't want to——

GERALD (*sharply*). I said—*quiet*.

HELLIWELL. Leave him be, Albert.

GERALD (*sits*). Thanks. Mind if I smoke now ?

(*All sit. With maddening slowness,* GERALD *takes out and lights a cigarette.* HELLIWELL *and* PARKER *watch him with impatience and look as if about to explode.*)

I went to North Wales for my holiday this summer——

HELLIWELL (*impatiently*). Is this part of it, 'cos *I* don't care *where* you went for your holidays ?

GERALD (*calmly*). I went to North Wales, and only came back about a fortnight ago. While I was there I made the acquaintance of a parson, who'd been in Africa for the last twenty years. When he learnt that I was the organist of Lane End Chapel, Clecklewyke, he became very excited, and then it turned out that he'd been at Lane End himself for a short time. About twenty-five years ago.

SOPPITT. What was his name ?

GERALD. Beech. Francis Edwin Beech.

HELLIWELL (*boisterously*). Oh—yes—Beech ! We were only talking about him to-night. We remember Mr. Beech. He married us, y'know. Yes, he married us, five-and-twenty years ago—all three couples. That's what we're celebrating—(*his voice suddenly dies away because he realizes what the other two have realized for the last minute that there might be something wrong. So as he mutters the end of his sentence now, he glances unhappily at the others*) y'know—being—married—twenty-five years——

(GERALD *looks at them over his cigarette.*)

PARKER (*swallowing*). Go on. Go on.

GERALD. I could see that something he remembered about Clecklewyke and Lane End worried him. (*With obvious relish.*) You might say, gentlemen, it was *preying* on his mind, it was *gnawing* at his conscience, it was *haunting* him, it was——

HELLIWELL (*angrily*). What is this—a recitation ?

GERALD. I must apologize if I'm boring you, gentlemen——

PARKER (*in sudden passion, jumping up*). La-di-dah ! La-di-dah ! (*He goes up stage, then turns down as* GERALD *stares at him in astonishment.*) Now if you've anything to tell us, for God's sake tell us—and don't la-di-dah ! (*He stands behind* HELLIWELL.)

HELLIWELL. Quite right, Albert. (*To* GERALD, *impatiently.*) Well, what did Mr. Beech say ?

GERALD. He didn't *say* anything.

(HELLIWELL *and* PARKER *are at once relieved and annoyed. They breathe more freely, but then feel they have been needlessly alarmed.* SOPPITT *waits to learn more and looks steadily at* GERALD.)

HELLIWELL. Well, what are you nattering on about him for—— ?

SOPPITT (*moving up to above the* R. *settee*). Just a minute, Joe. (*To* GERALD.) That's not all, is it ?

GERALD. All ? I should think not ! Only you won't give me a chance. I said he didn't *say* anything, but he *wrote* something. The letter only came two days ago. I have it here. (*He produces one rather small sheet of notepaper, written on both sides. He now reads it impressively.*) From the Reverend Francis Edwin Beech. " Dear Mr. Forbes. Before returning to Africa I feel I owe it both to you and to myself to explain what you must have found puzzling in my many references to Clecklewyke and Lane End Chapel. Although I was only temporarily at Lane End, I could not forget it, for there I was guilty of the most culpable negligence.

(*The three men look at one another.*)

I went to Clecklewyke straight from college, and during those first few months I did not realize that there were various forms I ought to have signed and had witnessed by church officers, so that one may be recorded as an authorized person to perform the ceremony of marriage——"

HELLIWELL (*rises, shouting*). What ? (*He grabs the letter from* GERALD, *stares at it, then reads himself, slowly.*) . . . " the ceremony of marriage. The result was, I was not then an authorized person. Fortunately during that short period I was only called upon twice to marry people, but the first time there were no less than three hopeful young couples who imagined— poor souls—that I was joining them in holy wedlock—when—I— was completely—unauthorized—to—do—so——"

PARKER (*crosses to* HELLIWELL, *yelling and snatching the letter.*) Let's have a look. (*He looks and* SOPPITT *joins him.*) It's signed all right too—Francis Edwin Beech.

GERALD (*rises*). And if you compare that signature with the one in the Chapel register, you'll see it's the same man. No deception. (*He moves away to* L.)

HELLIWELL (*dazed and bitter*). Why—the bloody donkey !

(*He sits down, dazed, on the upper end of the settee* L. *He and* PARKER *and* SOPPITT *look at one another in silent consternation.*)

SOPPITT (*slowly, thoughtfully*). Why, if we've never been married at all, then—— (*He goes to the upper end of the settee* R.)

HELLIWELL. Don't start working it out in detail, Herbert, 'cos it gets very ugly—very ugly. There's that lad o' yours at Grammar School, for instance—I wouldn't like to have to give 'im a name now——

SOPPITT (*indignantly*). Here, steady, Joe——

HELLIWELL. Well, you see, it gets very ugly. Keep your mind off t'details.

PARKER (*bitterly*). Silver wedding ! (*He sits in the chair* C.)

HELLIWELL. Now don't you start neither, Albert.

PARKER (*solemnly*). Joe, Herbert, when them three poor women upstairs gets to know what they really are——

HELLIWELL (*grimly*). Then t'balloon goes up properly. Talk about a rumpus. You'll 'ear 'em from 'ere to Leeds.

PARKER (*gravely*). Joe, Herbert, they mustn't know. Nobody must know. Why—we'd be laughed right out o' town. What—Alderman Helliwell—Councillor Albert Parker—Herbert Soppitt—all big men at Chapel, too ! I tell you, if this leaks out—we're done.

HELLIWELL. We are, Albert.

SOPPITT (*horrified*). If once it got into the papers !

HELLIWELL (*even more horrified*). Papers ! Oh—Christmas ! —it's got to be kept from t'papers.

(GERALD, *who has been leaving them to themselves to digest this news, now turns to them again, coming to* L.C.)

GERALD (*holding out his hand*). You'd better give me that letter, hadn't you ?

PARKER } (*together*). Oh no ! (*They both rise.*)
HELLIWELL }

(*They stand together as if protecting it.*)

PARKER (*holding it out*). This letter——

HELLIWELL (*snatching it*). Here——

PARKER (*angrily*). Nay, Joe—give it back——

HELLIWELL. I'm sorry, Albert, but I don't trust nobody wi' this letter but meself. Why—it's—it's dynamite !

GERALD. Yes, but it's addressed to me, and so it happens to be my property, you know.

SOPPITT. I'm afraid he's right there.

HELLIWELL (*turning on him, annoyed*). You would have to put that in, wouldn't you ? Dang me, you're in this mess just as we are, aren't you ?

PARKER (*severely*). Anyhow, *we've* a position to keep up even if you haven't, Herbert.

SOPPITT (*apologetically*). I was only saying he's right when he says it's his property. We had a case——

HELLIWELL (*aggressively*). Never mind about that case. Think about this case. It's a whole truck-load o' cases, this is. (*He turns up* C.)

GERALD. My letter, please.

(HELLIWELL *turns down to him.*)

HELLIWELL (*ingratiatingly*). Now listen, lad. I know you only want to do what's right. And we happened to be a bit 'asty with you, when you first came in. We didn't mean it. Just—a way o' talking. When Herbert Soppitt there gets started——

SOPPITT (*indignantly*). What—me!

PARKER (*severely*). You were 'asty, y'know, Herbert, you can't deny it. (*To* GERALD.) Mind you, I'll say now to your face what I've often said behind your back. You gave us best *Messiah* and best *Elijah* we've ever had at Lane End.

HELLIWELL. Easy, easy! Best i' Clecklewyke! And why? I've told 'em when they've asked me. " That young feller of ours is clever," I said. " I knew he had it in him," I said.

SOPPITT (*hopefully, rising*). Yes, you did, Joe. (*To* GERALD.) And so did I. I've always been on your side.

GERALD. I believe you have, Mr. Soppitt. (*To all three of them.*) You can keep that letter to-night—on one condition. That Mr. Soppitt has it.

SOPPITT (*eagerly, holding out his hand*). Thank you, Joe.

HELLIWELL (*uneasily*). What's the idea o' this? (*He backs up a little.*)

GERALD. That happens to be the way I feel about it. Now, either give it back to me at once—or hand it over to Mr. Soppitt, who'll be answerable to me for it.

SOPPITT (*eagerly*). Certainly, certainly.

(HELLIWELL *silently and grudgingly hands it over.* SOPPITT *puts it carefully in his inside pocket. The others watch him like hawks.* GERALD *moves to the window. There is a pause, then we hear a knocking from upstairs.*)

HELLIWELL. Knocking. (*Not happily.*)

PARKER (*grimly*). I 'eard.

HELLIWELL. That means she's getting impatient.

SOPPITT. I expect Clara's been ready to come down for some time.

HELLIWELL (*bitterly*). They want to get on with the celebration.

PARKER (*bitterly*). Chat about old times.

HELLIWELL (*bitterly*). Nice game o' cards.

GERALD (*after a pause*). I'd better be going. (*He moves up to the door.*)

HELLIWELL (*hastily going up to him*). No, no. No. Take it easy.

PARKER. No 'urry, no 'urry at all. I expect Joe has a nice cigar for you somewhere.

HELLIWELL (*with forced joviality*). Certainly I have. And a drink of anything you fancy——

GERALD. No, thanks. And I must be going.

(HELLIWELL *brings him down.*)

HELLIWELL. Now listen, lad. We've admitted we were 'asty with you, so just forget about it, will you? Now you see the mess we're in, through no fault of ours——

(*He goes up for his cigars.*)

GERALD. I do. And it *is* a mess, isn't it ? Especially when you begin to think——

PARKER (*hastily*). Yes, quite so, but don't you bother thinking. Just—(*rather desperately*) try an' forget you ever saw that letter.

HELLIWELL (*who now comes down* o. *with the cigars*). We're all friends, the best of friends. Now you've got to have a cigar or two, lad—I insist—(*he sticks several cigars into* GERALD's *outside pocket, as he talks*) and you're going to promise us—on your word of honour—not to tell anybody anything about this nasty business, aren't you ?

(*All three look at him anxiously. He keeps them waiting a moment or two.*)

GERALD. All right.

(*They breathe again.* HELLIWELL *shakes his hand.*)

HELLIWELL. And you won't regret it, lad.

(*The knocking from upstairs is heard again.*)

PARKER (*miserably*). 'Ear that.

HELLIWELL. It's wife again.

SOPPITT (*thoughtfully*). Curious thing about wives. They're always telling you what poor company you are for them, yet they're always wanting to get back to you.

HELLIWELL (*darkly*). That isn't 'cos they enjoy your company. It's so they can see what you're doing.

PARKER. Well, what are we doing ?

HELLIWELL (*sharply now*). Wasting time. (*To them.*) Now listen, chaps, we're in no proper shape yet to face t'wives. They'd have it all out of us in ten minutes, and then fat'll be in t'fire.

PARKER. I know. We've got to put our thinking caps on.

SOPPITT. I suppose Mr. Beech couldn't have been mistaken, could he ?

PARKER. We might take that letter and get expert advice——

HELLIWELL (*hastily*). What ! An' 'ave it all over the town.

PARKER (*quickly*). We might put a case—without mentioning names——

HELLIWELL (*with decision*). I know what we'll do. We'll nip down to t'club, 'cos we can talk it over there in peace an' quiet. Come on, chaps. Just as we are, straight down t'club. (*To* GERALD.) Now, young man, you promised. You won't go back on your word ?

GERALD. No. You're safe with me.

HELLIWELL (*urgently*). Good lad ! Now, wait till we've got off, then go out front way. Come on, Albert, Herbert, we've no time to lose an' we go this way—(*bustling them towards the exit* R. *through the conservatory*) straight to t'club.

(*They go out* R. GERALD *looks at his watch, smiles, lights a cigarette, then makes for the door, which has never been quite closed. When he opens it suddenly,* MRS. NORTHROP, *still holding a towel and a large glass dish, which she is wiping perfunctorily, is discovered just behind the door. She is in high glee and not at all abashed at being found there. She leans against the hinge of the door, and* GERALD *backs a little into the room.*)

GERALD (*with mock sternness*). Have you been listening ?

MRS. NORTHROP (*who may have had a drink or two*). Listening ! I should think I have been listening ! I wouldn't have missed this lot even if it means 'aving earache for a week. None of 'em rightly married at all ! Not one of 'em properly tied up ! (*She begins laughing quite suddenly, and then goes off into peals of laughter, rolling against the door. The dish she holds seems to be in danger.*)

GERALD (*amused as he goes past her, out*). Look out—or you may break that dish.

MRS. NORTHROP (*calling to him*). Brek a dish ! If I want to, I'll brek a dozen now.

GERALD (*just off, challengingly*). Not you ! I dare you !

MRS. NORTHROP (*coolly*). Well, here's a start, any road.

(*She tosses the dish down and it smashes noisily in the hall. We hear* GERALD *give a laughing shout, then bang the front door.* MRS. NORTHROP *now starts laughing helplessly again, still leaning against the door.*)

Nay—dammit !—— (*Laughing.*) Oh dear—oh dear—oh dear——

(*She is still roaring with laughter as—*

The CURTAIN *briskly descends.*)

ACT II

SCENE.—*The same, about half an hour later.*

The lights are on. MARIA *is drawing curtains,* ANNIE *and* CLARA *are laying out the cards and counters for Newmarket on a card table* C., *and they continue doing this throughout the scene that follows, chiefly counting the coloured counters and putting them into piles.*

CLARA (*with much discontent*). Well, I must say—this is a queer way o' going on.

MARIA. They'll have just gone outside to finish their smokes.

CLARA (*grimly*). When Herbert takes me out to enjoy myself, I don't expect him to be outside finishing any smokes.

ANNIE (*at table*). Perhaps they'd something they wanted to talk over.

CLARA. Well, they can talk it over here, can't they?

(RUBY *enters from the conservatory.*)

MARIA (*turning away from the window*). Well, Ruby, are they out there?

RUBY. No, they aren't.

MARIA (*sharply, moving to* L.C.). Have you looked properly?

RUBY. Well, I couldn't miss three grown men in a garden that size.

MARIA. Did you look up and down the road like I told you?

RUBY. Yes, but they aren't there.

(*The three wives look at one another, puzzled.*)

CLARA. Didn't you hear them go?

RUBY. No. I was back in t'kitchen all time, doing t'washing up. That Mrs. Northrop left me to it.

MARIA. Where was she, then?

RUBY. Out 'ere somewhere, I fancy. I know she's gone like a dafthead ever since she come back. Laughin' to herself—like a proper barmpot.

MARIA. Well, ask Mrs. Northrop if she knows where they went.

(RUBY *goes.* MARIA *comes to the* L. *of the* C. *table.*)

That noise you heard upstairs was a bit o' this Mrs. Northrop's work—one o' my best dishes gone. An' Ruby says she just laughed.

CLARA. Stop it out of her wages and see if she can get a good laugh out o' that. I've no patience with 'em.

ANNIE. I thought she didn't look a nice woman.

CLARA. One o' them idle drinking pieces o' nothing from back o' t'mill.

MARIA. Well, I was in a hurry and had to have somebody. But she goes—for good—to-night.

(RUBY *appears.*)

RUBY. Mrs. Northrop says they wanted to have a nice quiet talk, so they went down to their club.

(RUBY *disappears.* MARIA *sits on the settee* L.)

CLARA (*angrily*). Club! *Club!*

ANNIE. And to-night of all nights. (*She sits on the* R. *settee.*) I do think it's a shame.

MARIA (*indignantly*). I never 'eard o' such a thing in me life.

CLARA (*furiously, moving down* R.). *Club!* I'll club him.

ANNIE. Nay, I don't know what's come over 'em.

CLARA (*angrily*). I know what'll come over one of 'em. (*Turns up behind the* R. *settee.*)

MARIA. Perhaps there's something up.

CLARA (*to* C.). Something down you mean—ale, stout, an' whisky. Drinks all round! Money no object! (*She sits in a chair* C.)

MARIA. They're 'ere.

(*The three of them immediately sit bolt upright and look very frosty. The men file in from the conservatory, looking very sheepish.*)

HELLIWELL (*nervously*). Ay—well——

MARIA (*grimly*). Well, what?

HELLIWELL. Well—nowt—really.

SOPPITT (*nervously*). We didn't—er—think you'd be down yet. Did we, Joe? Did we, Albert?

HELLIWELL. No, we didn't, Herbert.

PARKER. That's right, we didn't.

CLARA (*cuttingly*). Herbert Soppitt, you must be wrong in your head. *Club!*

ANNIE. And to-night of all nights!

HELLIWELL. Well, you see, we thought we'd just nip down for a few minutes while you were talking upstairs.

MARIA. What for?

PARKER. Oh—just to talk over one or two things.

CLARA. What things?

SOPPITT. Oh—just—things, y'know—things in general.

(*He comes to the left of the* C. *chair, with* HELLIWELL.)

PARKER (*coming forward to the* R. *of the chair* C., *rubbing his hands*). Well—I see the table's all ready—so what about that nice little game o' Newmarket ?

CLARA. You'll get no Newmarket out o' me to-night.

ANNIE. You're—you're—selfish.

CLARA. Have you just found that out ? Never think about anything but their own comfort and convenience.

MARIA. I'm surprised at you, Joe Helliwell—and after I'd planned to make everything so nice.

CLARA. Lot o' thanks you get from them ! Club ! (*Looking hard at* SOPPITT.) Well, go on—say something.

(*The men look at one another uneasily. Then the women look indignantly.*)

ANNIE. Just think what day it is !

CLARA. And after giving you best years of our life—without a word o' thanks.

MARIA. An' just remember, Joe Helliwell, there were plenty of other fellows I could have had besides you.

ANNIE. You seem to think—once you've married us, you can take us for granted.

PARKER (*uneasily*). Nay, I don't.

CLARA (*very sharply*). Yes, you do—all alike !

MARIA. If some of you woke up to-morrow to find you weren't married to us, you'd be in for a few big surprises.

HELLIWELL (*uneasily*). Yes—I dare say—you're right.

MARIA (*staring at him*). Joe Helliwell, what's matter with you to-night ?

HELLIWELL (*uneasily*). Nowt—nowt's wrong wi' me, love.

CLARA (*looking hard at* SOPPITT). You'll hear more about this when I get you 'ome.

SOPPITT (*mildly*). Yes, Clara.

(*The women look at the men again, then at one another. Now they turn away from the men, ignoring them.*)

MARIA. What were you saying about your cousin, Clara ?

CLARA (*ignoring the men*). Oh—well, the doctor said, " You're all acid, Mrs. Foster, that's your trouble. You're making acid as fast as you can go."

ANNIE. Oh—poor thing !

CLARA. Yes, but it didn't surprise me, way she'd eat. I once saw her eat nine oyster patties, finishing 'em up after their Ethel got married. I said, " Nay, Edith, have a bit o' mercy on your inside," but of course she just laughed.

(*The men have been cautiously moving to the back towards the door. As* HELLIWELL *has his hand on the handle,* MARIA *turns on him.*)

MARIA. And where're you going now ?
HELLIWELL (*uneasily*). Into t'dining-room.
MARIA. What for ?
HELLIWELL. Well—because—well—— (*He gathers boldness.*)
We've summat to talk over. Albert, 'Erbert, quick !

(*They file out smartly, without looking behind them. The women stare at them in amazement. The door shuts. The women look at one another.*)

MARIA. Now what's come over 'em ?
ANNIE. There's something up.
CLARA. What can be up ? They're just acting stupid, that's all. But wait till I get his lordship 'ome.
ANNIE. Suppose we went home now——
CLARA. No fear ! That's just what they'd like. Back to t'club !
MARIA. I'd go up to bed now and lock me door, if I didn't think I'd be missing something.
ANNIE. It's a pity we can't go off just by ourselves—for a day or two.
CLARA. And what sort o' game are they going to get up to while we're gone ? But I've a good mind to go in and tell mine, " Look, I've been married to you for five-and-twenty years and it's about time I had a rest."
MARIA. And for two pins I'll say to Joe, " If you got down on your bended knees and begged me to, I wouldn't stay married to you if I didn't have to."

(*The door opens slowly, and* MRS. NORTHROP *comes just inside, carrying a large string-bag, with clothes, two stout bottles in, etc. She is dressed to go home now.*)

MRS. NORTHROP. I've done.
MARIA (*suspiciously*). It hasn't taken you very long.
MRS. NORTHROP (*modestly*). No—but then I'm a rare worker. Many a one's said to me, " Mrs. Northrop, I can't believe you've just that pair of 'ands—you're a wonder."
MARIA (*acidly*). Well, I don't think I want a wonder here, Mrs. Northrop. I'll pay you what I owe you to-night, and then you needn't come again.
MRS. NORTHROP (*bridling*). Ho, I see—that's it, is it ?
MARIA. Yes, it is. I don't consider you satisfactory.
CLARA. I should think not !
MRS. NORTHROP (*annoyed*). Who's askin' you to pass remarks ? (*To* MARIA.) And don't think I want to come 'ere again. Me 'usband wouldn't let me, anyhow, when he 'ears what I 'ave to tell him. We've always kept ourselves respectable.
MARIA. And what does that mean ?
CLARA. Don't encourage her impudence.

MRS. NORTHROP. An' *you* mind your own interference. (*To* MARIA.) I was beginnin' to feel sorry for you—but now——
MARIA (*coldly*). I don't know what you're talking about.
CLARA. What's she got in that bag ?
MRS. NORTHROP (*angrily*). I've got me old boots an' apron an' cleanin' stuff in this bag——
MARIA. I can see two bottles there——
MRS. NORTHROP (*angrily*). Well, what if you can ? D'you think you're the only folk i' Clecklewyke who can buy summat to sup ? If you must know, these is two stout empties I'm taking away 'cos they belong to me—bought an' paid for by me at Jackson's off-licence—an' if you don't believe me go an' ask 'em.
MARIA (*rises, stopping* CLARA *from bursting in*). No, Clara, let her alone—we've had enough. (*To* MRS. NORTHROP, *rather haughtily.*) It's twenty-four shillings altogether, isn't it ? (*She goes up to the bureau.*)
MRS. NORTHROP (*aggressively*). No, it isn't. It's twenty-five and six—if I never speak another word.
MARIA (*returns to the* L. *of* MRS. NORTHROP). All right then, twenty-five and six, but I'm going to take something off for that dish you broke——
MRS. NORTHROP (*angrily*). You won't take a damned ha'penny off !
CLARA. Language now as well as back answers !
MARIA (*giving* MRS. NORTHROP *a sovereign*). Here's a pound and that's all you'll get.
MRS. NORTHROP (*angrily*). I won't 'ave it. I won't 'ave it.
MARIA (*leaving it on the nearest table to* MRS. NORTHROP). There it is, Mrs. Northrop, and it's all you'll get. (*She sits down in stately fashion and turns to* CLARA.) Let's see, Clara, what were you saying ?

(*All three women now ignore* MRS. NORTHROP, *which makes her angrier than ever.*)

MRS. NORTHROP (*drowning any possible conversation*). An' don't sit there tryin' to look like duchesses, 'cos I've lived round 'ere too long an' I know too much about yer. Tryin' to swank ! Why (*pointing to* MARIA), I remember you when you were Maria Fawcett an' you were nobbut a burler and mender at Barkinson's afore you took up wi' Joe Helliwell, an' he were nobbut a woolsorter i' them days. And as for you (*pointing to* CLARA), I remember time when you were weighin' out apples an' potatoes in your father's greengrocer's shop, corner o' Park Road, an' a mucky little shop it wor an' all——
MARIA (*rising, angrily*). I'll fetch my husband.
MRS. NORTHROP. He isn't your husband. I was goin' to say I'm as good as you, but fact is I'm a damn' sight better, 'cos

I'm a respectable married woman an' that's more than any o'
you can say——

Clara (*angrily*). Get a policeman.

Mrs. Northrop (*derisively*). Get a policeman. Get a dozen,
an' they'll all 'ave a good laugh when they 'ear what I 'ave to
tell 'em. Not one o' you properly married at all. I 'eard that
organist o' yours tellin' your 'usbands—if I can call 'em your
'usbands. I wor just be'ind t'door—an' this lot wor too good to
miss—better than a turn at t'Empire.

Clara (*rising, angrily*). I don't believe a word of it.

Mrs. Northrop. Please yerself. But 'e give 'em a letter,
an' that's why they went down to t'club to talk it over—an' I
can't say I blame 'em, 'cos they've plenty to talk over. An', by
gow, so 'ave you three. It's about time yer thought o' getting
wed, isn't it ?

(*They stare in silence. She gives them a triumphant look, then
picks up her sovereign.*)

And now you owe me another five an' six at least—an' if you've
any sense you'll see I get it—but I can't stop no longer 'cos I've
said I meet me 'usband down at " 'Are an' 'Ounds," 'cos they're
'aving a draw for a goose for Clecklewyke Tide an' we've three
tickets—so I'll say *good night.*

(*She bangs the door. The three women stare at one another in
consternation.*)

Maria. That's why they were so queer. I knew there was
something.

Clara (*bitterly*). The daft blockheads ! (*To R. of the c. chair.*)

(Annie *suddenly begins laughing.*)

Oh—for goodness' sake, Annie Parker !

Annie (*still laughing*). I'm not Annie Parker. And it all
sounds so silly.

Maria (*indignantly*). Silly ! What's silly about it ? (*She
goes to the L. of* Clara.)

Clara (*bitterly*). Serves me right for ever bothering with
anybody so gormless. Isn't this Herbert Soppitt all over.
Couldn't even get us married right !

Maria (*sitting c., and looking distressed*). But—Clara, Annie—
this is *awful.* What are we going to do ?

Clara. I know what we're *not* going to do—and that's play
Newmarket. (*She begins putting things away, helped by the other
two.*)

Annie. Eee—we'll look awfully silly lining up at Lane End
Chapel again to get married, won't we ?

Clara (*angrily*). Oh—for goodness' sake——!

MARIA (*bitterly*). Better tell them three daftheads in t'dining-room to come in now.

CLARA. No, just a minute.

MARIA. What for ?

CLARA. 'Cos I want to think an' very sight of Herbert'll make me that mad I won't be able to think. (*She ponders for a moment.*) Now if nobody knew but us, it wouldn't matter so much.

MARIA. But that fool of a parson knows——

CLARA. And the organist knows——

ANNIE. And your Mrs. Northrop knows—don't forget that—and you wouldn't pay her that five-and-six——

MARIA. Here, one o' them men must fetch her back.

CLARA. I should think so. Why, if people get to know about this—we're—we're——

RUBY (*looking in, announcing loudly*). " Yorkshire Argus."

CLARA (*in a panic*). We don't want any " Yorkshire Argus " here—or God knows where we'll be——

(*She is interrupted by the entrance of* FRED DYSON, *who has had some drinks and is pleased with himself.*)

DYSON (*very heartily*). Well, here we are again. At least I am. Fred Dyson—" Yorkshire Argus." Mrs. Helliwell ?

MARIA (*rather faintly*). Yes.

DYSON (*same tone*). And Mrs. Albert Parker and Mrs. Soppitt —three lucky ladies, eh ?

(*They are looking anything but fortunate.*)

Now, you'd never guess my trouble.

ANNIE (*who can't resist it*). You'd never guess ours, either.

MARIA (*hastily*). Shut up, Annie. What were you saying, Mr. Dyson ?

DYSON. I've gone and lost our photographer—Henry Ormonroyd. Brought him with me here earlier on, then we went back to the " Lion," where he'd met an old pal. I left 'em singing " Larboard Watch " in the tap-room, not twenty minutes since, went into the private bar five minutes afterwards, couldn't find old Henry anywhere, so thought he must have come up here. By the way, where's the party ?

ANNIE. This is it.

MARIA (*hastily*). Shut up, Annie. (*Rather desperately, to* DYSON.) You see, my husband—Alderman Helliwell—you know him, of course ?

DYSON (*heartily*). Certainly. He's quite a public figure, these days. That's why the " Argus " sent me up here to-night—when he told 'em you were all celebrating your silver wedding——

CLARA (*unpleasantly*). Oh—he suggested your coming here, did he ?

DYSON. He did.

CLARA (*unpleasantly*). He would!

MARIA. Well, he didn't know then—what—I mean—— (*Her voice falters and dies away.*)

DYSON. Our readers 'ud like to know all about this affair.

CLARA (*grimly*). An' I'll bet they would!

MARIA. Now 'ave a bit o' sense, Clara——

CLARA (*quickly*). Why, you nearly gave it away——

ANNIE (*coming in*). What on earth are you saying, you two ? (*She smiles at* DYSON, *who is looking rather mystified.*) It's all right, Mr. Dyson. What Mrs. Helliwell was going to say was that there was only just us six, y'know. It wasn't a real party. Just a little—er—private—er—sort of—you know.

DYSON (*looking about him, thirstily*). I know. Just a cosy little do—with—er—a few drinks——

MARIA. That's it.

DYSON. A few drinks—and—er—cigars—and—er—so on.

(*But they do not take the hint, so now he pulls out a pencil and a bit of paper.*)

Now, Mrs. Helliwell, wouldn't you like to tell our readers just what your feelings are now that you're celebrating twenty-five years of happy marriage ?

MARIA (*her face working*). I—er—I—er——

DYSON. You needn't be shy, Mrs. Helliwell. Now, come on.

(*To his astonishment,* MARIA *suddenly bursts into tears, and then hurries out of the room.*)

CLARA (*reproachfully*). Now, look what you've done, young man.

DYSON (*astonished*). Nay, dash it—what have I done ? I only asked her——

ANNIE (*hastily*). She's a bit upset to-night—you know, what with all the excitement. It's no use your staying now—you'd better go and find your photographer.

CLARA (*angrily*). Now, Annie, for goodness' sake ! We want no photographers here.

ANNIE (*to* DYSON). That's all right. She's upset too. Now you just pop off.

(ANNIE *almost marches* DYSON *to the door and sees him through it. We hear him go out.* CLARA *sits breathing very hard.* ANNIE *returns, leaving door open behind her.*)

Well, we're rid of him.

CLARA (R.C.). For how long ?

ANNIE (*annoyed*). You can't sit there, Clara, just saying " For how long ? " as if you're paying me to manage this business. If we want it kept quiet, we'll have to stir ourselves and

not sit about shouting and nearly giving it all away as you and
Maria did when that chap was here.

CLARA (*bitterly*). If we hadn't said we'd marry a set o' num-
skulls, this would never 'ave happened. If my poor mother was
alive to see this day——

(MARIA *returns, blowing her nose, and sits down miserably
on the* L. *settee.*)

MARIA (*unhappily*). I'm sorry—Clara, Annie—but I just
couldn't help it. When he asked me that question, something
turned right over inside—an' next minute I was crying.

CLARA (*severely*). Well, crying's not going to get us out of
this mess.

ANNIE (*sharply*). You're never satisfied, Clara. First you
go on at me for laughing and now you blame poor Maria for
crying—— (*She sits* C.)

CLARA (*loudly, sharply*). Well, what do you want to go
laughing an' crying for ? What do you think this is ? " Uncle
Tom's Cabin " ? (*She sits on the* R. *settee.*)

MARIA. They're coming in.

(*The women sit back, grimly waiting.* HELLIWELL, PARKER,
SOPPITT *enter, and the women look at them.* SOPPITT *drops
down* R. PARKER *comes* R.C., *with* HELLIWELL *on his* L.)

PARKER (*uneasily*). Who was that ?

(*No reply. He exchanges a glance with* SOPPITT *and* HELLIWELL.)

I said, who was it came just then ?

CLARA (*suddenly, fiercely*). " Yorkshire Argus ! "

PARKER (*resigned tone*). They know.

ANNIE (*sharply*). 'Course we know.

(HELLIWELL *looks at them, then makes for the door again.*)

MARIA. And where are you going ?

HELLIWELL. To fetch t'whisky ?

MARIA. And is whisky going to 'elp us ?

HELLIWELL. I don't know about you, but it'll help me.
(*He goes out.*)

MARIA (*hopefully*). It's not all a tale, is it ?

PARKER. No, it's right enough. We put case to a chap at
club—no names, of course—and he said it 'ad 'appened a few
times—when a young parson thought he was qualified to marry
folk—an' it turned out he wasn't. But of course it 'asn't happened often.

CLARA. No, but it has to 'appen to *us.* (*Fiercely to* SOPPITT.)
1 blame you for this.

SOPPITT (*unhappily to* PARKER). Didn't I tell you she would ?

CLARA (*sharply*). *She!* Who's *she*? The cat? Just remember you're talking about your own wife.

PARKER. Ah—but you see, he isn't—not now.

CLARA (*angrily*). Now, stop that, Albert Parker.

(HELLIWELL *returns with a large tray, with whisky, soda and glasses.*)

HELLIWELL. Any lady like a drop?

MARIA. State I'm in now, it 'ud choke me.

(*The other women shake their heads scornfully.*)

HELLIWELL. Albert?

PARKER. Thanks, I think I will, Joe. (*He goes to him.*)

HELLIWELL (*busy with drinks*). 'Erbert?

CLARA (*quickly*). He mustn't 'ave any.

HELLIWELL. 'Erbert?

CLARA (*confidently*). You 'eard what I said, Herbert. You're not to 'ave any.

SOPPITT (*the rebel now*). Thanks, Joe, just a drop.

(*He goes up, looks at his wife as he takes his glass and drinks, then comes away, still looking at her, while she glares at him.*)

HELLIWELL. 'Ere, but I'd never ha' thought young Forbes 'ud have back on his word like that, when he promised solemnly not to tell another soul.

MARIA. But he didn't tell us.

HELLIWELL (*staggered*). Eh? (*He exchanges an alarmed glance with the other men.*) Who did, then?

MARIA. Charwoman—Mrs. Northrop. She 'eard you, behind that door.

HELLIWELL (*alarmed*). 'Ere, where is she?

MARIA. Gone.

ANNIE (*with some malice as she rises, moving to the* R. *settee*). Maria's just given her the push.

PARKER (*angrily*). If she's gone off with this news you just might as well play it on Town Hall chimes.

HELLIWELL (*angrily*). Why didn't you say so at first? If this woman gets round wi' this tale about us, we'll never live it down. Did she go 'ome?

ANNIE. No, to the "Hare and Hounds." (*She sits* L. *of* CLARA.)

HELLIWELL (*masterfully*). Herbert, swallow that whisky quick —an' nip down to t'"Hare an' Hounds" as fast as you can go, an' bring her back——

SOPPITT. But I don't know her.

HELLIWELL. Nay, damn it, you saw her in here, not an hour since——

SOPPITT. An' she doesn't know me.

HELLIWELL. Now, don't make difficulties, Herbert. Off you go. (*He moves him towards the conservatory.*) And bring her back as fast as you can and promise her owt she asks so long as you get back. (*He is now outside, shouting.*) An' make haste. We're depending on you.

(HELLIWELL *returns, blowing, carrying* SOPPITT'S *glass. He is about to drink out of this when he remembers, so he takes and drinks from his own, then breathes noisily and mops his brow. They are all quiet for a moment.*)

You know, Albert lad, it feels quite peculiar to me.

PARKER. What does ?

HELLIWELL. This—not being married.

MARIA (*rising, solemn*). Joe Helliwell, 'ow can you stand there an' say a thing like that ?

CLARA } (*together*). { He ought to be ashamed of himself.
ANNIE }   { I'm surprised at you, Joe.

HELLIWELL (*bewildered*). What—what are you talking about ?

MARIA (*solemnly*). After twenty-five years together. Haven't I been a good wife to you, Joe Helliwell ?

HELLIWELL. Well, I'm not complaining, am I ?

PARKER (*tactlessly*). You've been the *same* as a good wife to him, Maria.

MARIA (*furiously*). The *same* ! I haven't been the same as a good wife, I've been a good wife, let me tell you, Albert Parker.

ANNIE } (*together*). { Nay, Albert !
CLARA }   { I never 'eard such silly talk.

PARKER (*aggressively*). Oh—an' what's silly about it, eh ?

CLARA. Everything.

HELLIWELL (*tactlessly*). Nay, but when you come to think of it—Albert's right.

PARKER (*solemn and fatuous*). We must face facts. Now, Maria, you might *feel* married to him——

MARIA (*scornfully*). I might *feel* married to him ! If you'd had twenty-five years of him, you wouldn't talk about *might.* Haven't I——   ◆

HELLIWELL (*cutting in noisily*). 'Ere, steady on, steady on— with your *twenty-five years of 'im.* Talking about me as if I were a dose o' typhoid fever.

MARIA (*loudly*). I'm not, Joe. All I'm saying is——

PARKER (*still louder*). Now let me finish what I started to say. I said—you might *feel* married to him—but strictly speaking— and in the eyes of the law—the fact is, you're *not* married to him. We're none of us married.

CLARA (*bitterly*). Some o' t'neighbours ha' missed it, couldn't you shout it louder ?

PARKER. I wasn't that loud.

HELLIWELL (*reproachfully*). You were bawling your 'ead off.

ANNIE. Yes, you were.

MARIA (*reproachfully*). You don't know who's listening. I'm surprised you haven't more sense, Albert.

PARKER (*irritably*). All right, all right, all right. But we shan't get anywhere till we face facts. It's not our fault, but our misfortune.

MARIA. I don't know so much about that either.

HELLIWELL. Oh ? (*To* ALBERT.) Goin' to blame us now.

MARIA. Well, an' why not ?

HELLIWELL (*irritably*). Nay, damn it—it wasn't *our* fault.

MARIA. If a chap asks me to marry him and then he takes me to chapel and puts me in front of a parson, I expect parson to be a real one an' not just somebody dressed up.

HELLIWELL. Well, don't I ?

MARIA. You should ha' found out.

HELLIWELL. Talk sense ! 'Ow could I know he wasn't properly qualified ?

MARIA (*sneering*). Well, it's funny it's got to 'appen to us, isn't it ?

PARKER. But that's what I say—it's not our fault, it's our misfortune. It's no use blaming anybody. Just couldn't be 'elped. But fact remains—we're——

CLARA (*interrupting angrily*). If you say it again, Albert Parker, I'll throw something at yer. You needn't go on and on about it.

MARIA (*bitterly*). Mostly at top o' your voice.

PARKER (*with an air of wounded dignity*). Say no more. I've finished. (*He turns his back on them.*)

(*All three women look at him disgustedly.* MARIA *now turns to* HELLIWELL.)

MARIA. But, Joe, you're not going to tell me you feel different —just because of this—this accident ?

HELLIWELL (*solemnly*). I won't tell you a lie, love. I can't help it, but ever since I've known I'm not married I've felt *most peculiar*.

MARIA (*rising, in a sudden temper*). Oo, I could knock your fat head off. (*She goes hurriedly to the door, making a sobbing noise on the way, and hurries out.*)

ANNIE (*rising, follows her*). Oh—poor Maria ! (*She goes out, closing the door.*)

CLARA. Well, I 'ope you're pleased with yourself now.

HELLIWELL (*sententiously*). Never interfere between 'usband and wife.

CLARA. You just said you weren't 'usband an' wife.

HELLIWELL (*angrily*). 'Ere, if I'm going to argue with a woman it might as well be the one I live with. (*He hurries out.*)

(*A silence.* PARKER *remains sulky and detached.*)

CLARA (*after a pause*). Well, after all these ructions, another glass o' port wouldn't do me any 'arm—(*she waits, then as there is no move from* PARKER)—thank you very much. (*She rises, with dignity, to help herself at the buffet up* R.C.) Nice manners we're being shown, I must say. (*She fills her glass.*) I said *nice manners*, Councillor Albert Parker! (*She comes down to the chair* C.)

PARKER (*turning, angrily*). Now if I were poor Herbert Soppitt, I'd think twice before I asked you to marry me again.

CLARA (*just going to drink*). Ask me again! There'll be no asking. Herbert Soppitt's my husband—an' he stays my husband.

PARKER. In the eyes of the law——

CLARA (*cutting in ruthlessly*). You said that before. But let me tell you, in the sight of Heaven Herbert and me's been married for twenty-five years.

PARKER (*triumphantly*). And there you're wrong again, because in the sight of Heaven nobody's married at all——

(HELLIWELL *pops his head in the doorway* L., *looking worried.*)

HELLIWELL. Just come in the dining-room a minute, Albert. We're having a bit of an argument——

PARKER. Yes, Joe.

(HELLIWELL *disappears.* PARKER *goes out, leaving the door a little open.* CLARA, *left alone, finishes her port, crosses* L.C., *then picks up the old photograph and glares with contempt at the figures on it. A house-bell can be heard ringing distantly now.*)

CLARA (*muttering her profound contempt at the figures in the photograph*). Yer silly young softheads! (*She bangs it down in some prominent place, face up.*)

(RUBY *now looks in.*)

RUBY. Mrs. Soppitt——

CLARA (*rather eagerly*). Yes?

RUBY. Mrs. Helliwell says will you go into t'dining-room. (*As* CLARA *moves quickly towards the door,* RUBY *adds coolly :*) Aaa—they're fratchin' like mad.

(CLARA *goes out quickly, followed by* RUBY. *We hear in the distance the sound of a door opening, the voices of the three in the dining-room noisily raised in argument, the shutting of the door, then a moment's silence. Then several sharp rings at the front door. After a moment,* RUBY'S *voice off, but coming nearer.*)

(*Off.*) Yes, I know. . . . All right. . . . 'Ere, mind them things. . . . This way. . . .

(RUBY *ushers in* ORMONROYD, *who is carrying his camera, etc., and is now very ripe.*)

ORMONROYD (*advances into the room and looks about him with great care, then returns to* RUBY.) Nobody here. (*He gives another glance to make sure.*) Nobody at all.

RUBY (*up* L.C.). They'll all be back again soon. They're mostly in dining-room—fratchin'.

ORMONROYD (C.). What—on a festive occasion like this ?

RUBY. That's right.

ORMONROYD. Well, it just shows you what human nature is. (*He wanders to* R.C.) Human nature ! T-t-t-t-t-t. I'll bet if it had been a funeral—they'd have all been in here, laughing their heads off. (*He looks closely at the cigars on the table* R.C.) There isn't such a thing as a cigar here, is there ?

RUBY (*moving down* C.). Yes, yer looking at 'em. D'you want one ? 'Ere. (*As he lights it.*) Me mother says if God had intended men to smoke He'd havé put chimneys in their heads.

ORMONROYD (*comes to her* R.). Tell your mother from me that if God had intended men to wear collars He'd have put collar-studs at back of their necks. (*He stares at her.*) What are you bobbing up an' down like that for ?

RUBY. I'm not bobbing up an' down. It's you. (*She laughs and regards him critically.*) You're a bit tiddly, aren't yer ?

ORMONROYD (*horror-struck*). Tidd-ldly ?

RUBY. Yes. Squiffy.

ORMONROYD (*surveying her mistily*). What an ex't'rornry idea ! You seem to me a mos' ex't'rornry sort of—little—well, I dunno, really—what's your name ?

RUBY. Ruby Birtle.

ORMONROYD (*tasting it*). Umm—Ruby——

RUBY. All right, I know it's a silly daft name, you can't tell me nowt about Ruby I 'aven't been told already—so don't try.

ORMONROYD (*solemnly*). Ruby, I think you're quite ex't'rornry. How old are you ?

RUBY (*quickly*). Fifteen—how old are you ?

ORMONROYD (*waving a hand, vaguely*). Thousands of years, thousands and thousands of years. (*He turns away* R.)

RUBY (*coolly*). You look to me about seventy.

ORMONROYD (*turns back, horrified*). Seventy ! I'm fifty-four.

RUBY (*severely*). Then you've been neglectin' yerself.

(ORMONROYD *looks at her, breathing hard and noisily.*)

Too much liftin' o' t'elbow.

ORMONROYD (*after indignant pause*). Do you ever read the " Police News " ?

RUBY. Yes. I like it. All 'orrible murders.

ORMONROYD. Then you must have seen them pictures of women who've been chopped up by their husbands——

RUBY (*with gusto*). Yes—with bloody 'atchets.

ORMONROYD (*impressively*). Well, if you don't look out, Ruby, you'll grow up to be one of them women. (*He wanders away* L., *and then notices and takes up the old photograph.*)

RUBY (*looking at it*). Aaaaa !—don't they look soft ? (*She looks suspiciously at him, dubiously.*) How d'you mean—one o' them women ?

ORMONROYD. Don't you bother about that, Ruby, you've plenty of time yet. (*He puts photograph down.*)

RUBY (*puzzled*). Time for what ?

ORMONROYD (*goes up* R.C., *intent on his art now*). Now what I'm going to do—is to take a flashlight group of the three couples —just as they were in the old photograph. Now—let me see—— (*Very solemnly and elaborately he sets up his camera, up stage* R., *then comes down and puts a chair facing it nearly centre.*)

RUBY (*who has been thinking*). 'Ere, d'you mean I've plenty of time yet to grow up an' then be chopped up ?

ORMONROYD (*absently*). Yes.

RUBY (*persistently*). But what would 'e want to chop me up for ?

ORMONROYD. Now you sit there a minute.

RUBY. I said, what would 'e want to chop me up for ?

ORMONROYD (*putting her into the chair and patting her shoulder*). Perhaps you might find one who wouldn't, but you'll have to be careful. Now you stay there, Ruby.

RUBY (*hopefully*). Are yer goin' to take my photo ?

ORMONROYD (*grimly*). Not for a few years—yet—— (*He is now fiddling with his camera.*)

RUBY (*after thoughtful pause*). D'you mean you're waiting for me to be chopped up ?

(*Throughout the dialogue that follows,* ORMONROYD *keeps looking through his lens or, with the assistance of* RUBY, *moves the chairs —or chairs and a settee—for the group of six who will face the camera. He also keeps putting* RUBY, *who always sits stiffly smiling, no matter what she may be saying at the time, in the various positions in the group to see how he can focus her.*)

(*Cheerfully, not reproachfully.*) Eeeee !—you've got a right nasty mind, 'aven't you ? (*A pause.*) Are *you* married ?

ORMONROYD. Yes.

RUBY. Yer wife doesn't seem to take much interest in yer.

ORMONROYD. How do you know ?

RUBY. Well, I'll bet yer clothes hasn't been brushed for a month. (*Going on cheerfully.*) Yer could almost make a meal off yer waistcoat—there's so much egg on it. (*After a pause.*) Why doesn't she tidy you up a bit ?

ORMONROYD (*busy with his preparations*). Because she's not here to do it.

RUBY. Doesn't she live with yer ?

ORMONROYD (*stopping to stare at her, with dignity*). Is it—er—essential—you should know all about my—er—private affairs ?

RUBY. Go on, yer might as well tell me. Where is she ?

ORMONROYD. Mrs. Ormonroyd at present is—er—helping her sister to run a boarding-house called " Palm View "—though the only palm you see there is the one my sister-in-law holds out.

RUBY. Where ? Blackpool ?

ORMONROYD. Not likely. There's a place you go to live in —not to die in. No, they're at Torquay. (*With profound scorn.*) *Torquay !*

RUBY (*impressed*). That's right down south, isn't it ?

ORMONROYD (*with mock pompousness*). Yes, my girl, Torquay is on the south coast of Devonshire. It is sheltered from the northerly and easterly winds, is open to the warm sea breezes from the south, and so is a favourite all-year-round resort of many delicate and refined persons of genteel society. In other words, it's a damned miserable hole. (*He surveys his arrangements with satisfaction.*) There we are, all ready for the three happy couples.

RUBY (*sceptically*). Did yer say 'appy ?

ORMONROYD. Why not ?

RUBY. Well, for a start, go an' listen to them four in t'dining-room.

ORMONROYD (*beginning solemnly*). Believe me, Rosie——

RUBY (*sharply*). Ruby.

ORMONROYD. Ruby. Believe me, you're still too young to understand.

RUBY. I've 'eard that afore, but nobody ever tells what it is I'm too young to understand. An' for years me brother kept rabbits.

ORMONROYD (*solemnly but vaguely*). It's not a question of rabbits—thank God ! But marriage—marriage—well, it's a very peculiar thing. There's parts of it I never much cared about myself.

RUBY. Which parts ?

ORMONROYD. Well—now I'm a man who likes a bit o' company. An' I like an occasional friendly glass. I'll admit it—I like an occasional friendly glass.

RUBY. It 'ud be all t'same if you didn't admit it. We could tell. (*Sniffs.*)

ORMONROYD. If these three couples here have been married for twenty-five years and—er—they're still sticking it, well, then I call 'em three happy couples, an' I won't listen to you or anybody else saying they're not. No, I won't have it. And if you or anybody else says, " Drink their health," I say, " Certainly, certainly, with pleasure." (*He gives himself a whisky and soda with remarkable speed.*) Wouldn't dare to refuse, 'cos it would be dead against my principles. Their very good health. (*He takes an enormous drink.*)

RUBY. Eeee!—you are goin' to be tiddly.

ORMONROYD (*ignoring this, if he heard it, and very mellow and sentimental now*). Ah—yes. To be together—side-by-side—through all life's sunshine and storms—hand-in-hand—in good times and bad ones—with always a loving smile—— (*Waving hand with cigar in.*)

RUBY (*coldly*). Mind yer cigar!

ORMONROYD. In sickness and in health—rich or poor—still together—side-by-side—hand-in-hand—through all life's sunshine and storms——

RUBY (*quickly*). You said that once.

ORMONROYD. Oh—yes—it's a wonderful—it's a bee-yutiful thing——

RUBY. What is?

ORMONROYD. *What is!* Lord help us—it's like talking to a little crocodile! I say—that it's a wonderful and bee-yutiful thing to go through good times and bad ones—always together—always with a loving smile——

RUBY. Side-by-side—an' 'and-in-'and——

ORMONROYD. Yes, and that's what I say.

RUBY. Then there must be summat wrong wi' me 'cos when I've tried goin' side-by-side an' 'and-in-'and even for twenty minutes I've 'ad more than I want.

ORMONROYD (*staring at her*). Extr'ord'n'ry! What's your name?

RUBY. It's still Ruby Birtle.

ORMONROYD. Well, haven't you had a home?

RUBY. 'Course I've 'ad a home. Why?

ORMONROYD. You talk as if you'd been brought up in a tram-shed. No sentiment. No tender feeling. No—no—poetry——

RUBY (*indignantly*). Go on. I know poetry. We learnt it at school. 'Ere——

(RUBY *recites, as* ORMONROYD *sits.*)

They grew in beauty side by side,
  They filled one home with glee;
Their graves are severed, far an' wide,
  By mount and stream and sea.

The same fond mother bent at night
  O'er each fair sleeping brow;
She 'ad each folder flower in sight—
  Where are those dreamers now?

One 'midst the forest of the west,
  By a dark stream is laid—
The Indian knows his place of rest
  Far——

(She hesitates. CLARA *enters quietly and stares at her in astonishment.* RUBY *gives her one startled look, then concludes hurriedly.)*

      —Far in the cedar shade.

*(*RUBY *hurries out.* CLARA *stands in* RUBY'S *place* L.C., ORMONROYD, *who has turned away and closed his eyes, now turns and opens them, astonished to see* CLARA *there.)*

ORMONROYD *(bewildered).* Now I call that most peculiar, *most* peculiar. I don't think I'm very well to-night——

CLARA *(same tone as* RUBY *used).* You're a bit tiddly, aren't you ?

ORMONROYD. Things aren't rightly in their place—if you know what I mean—but I'll get it——

CLARA. Who are you, and what are you doing here ?

ORMONROYD *(still dazed).* Henry Ormonroyd—" Yorkshire Argus "—take picture—silver wedding group——

CLARA *(firmly).* There's no silver wedding group'll be taken *here* to-night.

ORMONROYD. Have I come to t'wrong house ?

CLARA *(firmly).* Yes. *(She crosses* R.)

ORMONROYD. Excuse me . . . *(Moving to the door up* L.C., *which opens to admit* ANNIE.)

ANNIE. Who's this ? *(She comes down* L.C.)

ORMONROYD *(hastily confused).* Nobody, nobody—I'll get it all straightened out in a minute—now give me time——

      *(*ORMONROYD *goes out.)*

ANNIE. Isn't he the *photographer* ?

CLARA *(bitterly).* Yes, an' he's drunk, an' when I come in, Maria's servant reciting poetry to him, an' God knows what's become of Herbert an' Albert an' that Mrs. Northrop an' *(angrily)* I'm fast losing my patience, I'm fast losing my patience——

ANNIE *(comes* R.C.). Now, Clara—— *(She turns as* MARIA *enters, rather wearily.)* Well, Maria ?

MARIA. I can't knock any sense at all into Joe. Where's Herbert ? *(To* L. *of* C. *chair.)*

CLARA *(grimly).* Still looking for that Mrs. Northrop. *(The front-door bell rings.)* Somebody else here now. *(She crosses* L., *sits on the settee.)*

MARIA. Well, don't carry on like that, Clara. I didn't ask 'em to come, whoever it is. *(She sits* C.)

CLARA. If you didn't, I'll bet Joe did. With his " Yorkshire Argus " !

      *(*RUBY *enters, rather mysteriously.)*

MARIA. Well, Ruby, who is it ?

RUBY (*lowering voice*). It's a woman.
CLARA (*hastily*). What woman ?

(ANNIE *drops a little down* R.C.)

MARIA. Now, Clara ! (*To* RUBY.) What sort of woman ?
Who is it ?
RUBY (*coming down* L. *of* MARIA, *confidentially*). I don't know.
But she doesn't look up to much to me. Paint on her face. An'
I believe her 'air's dyed.

(*The three women look at one another.*)

CLARA (*primly*). We don't want that sort o' woman here,
Maria.
MARIA. 'Course we don't—but—— (*She hesitates.*)
ANNIE. You'll have to see what she wants, Maria. It might
be something to do with—y'know—this business.
CLARA (*angrily*). How could it be ?
ANNIE. Well, you never know, do yer ?
CLARA. Let Joe see what she wants.
MARIA (*rising,* L. *of chair*). Oh—no—state of mind Joe's in,
I'd better see her. Ask her to come in, Ruby—and—er—you
needn't bother Mr. Helliwell just now. (*She crosses* L., *sits* R. *of*
CLARA.)

(RUBY *goes out. The three women settle themselves, rather anxiously.*
RUBY *ushers in* LOTTIE, *who enters smiling broadly.* MARIA
rises, the other two remaining seated.)

MARIA (*nervously*). Good evening.
LOTTIE (L.C.). Good evening.
MARIA. Did you want to see me ?
LOTTIE (*coolly, crossing to the chair* C.). No, not particularly.
(*She sits down, calmly, and looks about her.*)

(*The other three women exchange puzzled glances.*)

MARIA. Er—I don't think I got your name.
LOTTIE. No. You didn't get it because I didn't give it. But
I'm Miss Lottie Grady.
MARIA (*with dignity*). And I'm Mrs. Helliwell.
LOTTIE (*shaking her head*). *No,* if we're all going to be on
our dignity, let's get it right. *You're not Mrs. Helliwell.* You're
Miss Maria Fawcett.
CLARA (*as* MARIA *is too stunned to speak*). Now just a minute
——
LOTTIE (*turning to her, with mock sweetness*). Miss Clara Gaw-
thorpe, isn't it ? Gawthorpe's, Greengrocer's, corner of Park
Road. (*Turning to* ANNIE.) I'm afraid I don't know *your*
maiden name——

ANNIE. I'm Mrs. Parker to you.

LOTTIE. Please yourself, I don't care.

(MARIA *sits on the* L. *settee.*)

I'm *broad-minded.* (*Surveying them with a smile.*)

CLARA (*angrily*). I suppose that Mrs. Northrop's been talking to you.

LOTTIE. Certainly. Met in the old "Hare and Hounds," where I used to work. She's an old friend of mine.

CLARA (*angrily*). If you've come 'ere to get money out of us——

LOTTIE. Who said anything about money ?

MARIA. Well, you must have some idea in coming to see us.

LOTTIE (*coolly*). Oh—I didn't come here to see any of you three. (*She turns her face to* ANNIE.)

ANNIE. Well, who did you come to see, then ?

LOTTIE (*smiling*). A gentleman friend, love.

CLARA (*angrily, rising*). *Gentleman friend !* (*She crosses down to below the* L. *settee.*) *You'll* find none o' your gentleman friends in *this* house, will she, Maria ?

MARIA (*indignantly*). I should think not !

ANNIE (*rising, goes to* R. *of* LOTTIE). Just a minute, Clara. I'd like to hear a bit more about this.

LOTTIE. Very sensible of you. You see, if a gentleman friend gets fond of me—then tells me—more than once—that if he wasn't married already, he'd marry me——

(MARIA *rises. A slight pause.*)

CLARA (*grimly*). Well, go on.

LOTTIE. Well—then I suddenly find out that he isn't married already, after all, then you can't blame me—can you ?—if I'd like to know if he's still in the same mind. (*She beams upon them, while they look at one another in growing consternation.*)

CLARA (*astounded*). Well, I'll be hanged ! (*She moves behind the* L. *settee.*)

ANNIE. Now we *are* getting to know something. (*She returns to the* R. *settee, sits.*)

MARIA (*flustered*). Clara—Annie. (*Suddenly crossing to* LOTTIE.) Who was it ?

(*The front-door bell rings.*)

ANNIE (*anxiously*). Just a minute, Maria, there's somebody else here now. (*Crossing* L. *to above* CLARA.)

CLARA (*angrily*). Oh, for goodness' sake—can't you keep 'em out ?

RUBY (*appearing, importantly*). The Rev-erent Clem-ent Mer-cer !

(*All three wives look startled.* MARIA *crosses back to the* L. *settee.* MERCER, *a large grave clergyman, enters, and* RUBY *retires.*)

MERCER (*sympathetically*).   Mrs. Helliwell ?   (*Down to* MARIA.)
MARIA (*faintly*).   Yes ?
MERCER (*taking her hand a moment*).   Now, Mrs. Helliwell, although you're not a member of my congregation, I want you to realize that I feel it my duty to give you any help I can.
MARIA (*confused*).   I'm afraid—I don't understand—Mr. Mercer.
MERCER.   Now, now, Mrs. Helliwell, don't worry.   Let's take everything calmly.   May I sit down ?

(MERCER *brings down the chair from the bureau up* L., *to* L.C., *and sits down, smiling at them.* MARIA *sits.*)

ANNIE.   Did somebody ask you to come here ?
MERCER.   Yes, madam.

(ANNIE *sits below* MARIA.)

A working man I know called Northrop stopped me in the street and told me to go at once to Alderman Helliwell's house as a clergyman's presence was urgently required here.   So here I am—entirely at your service.

(LOTTIE *in danger of exploding rises and goes quickly towards the conservatory, where she stands with her back to the others.* MERCER *gives her a puzzled glance, then turns to the other three.*)

Now, what is it ?   Not, I hope, a really dangerous illness ?
MARIA (*blankly*).   No.
MERCER (*rather puzzled*).   Ah !—I hurried because I thought there might be.   But perhaps you feel some younger member of your family is in urgent need of spiritual guidance.   An erring son or daughter ?

(*A noise from* LOTTIE.)

CLARA (*forcefully*).   No.
MERCER (*puzzled*).   I beg your pardon ?
CLARA.   I just said No.   I mean, there aren't any erring sons and daughters.   Just husbands, that's all.
MERCER (*rises*).   Husbands ?

(LOTTIE *suddenly bursts into a peal of laughter, turning towards them.* MERCER *looks at her, puzzled.*)

LOTTIE (*crosses to* R. *of the chair* C., *laughing*).   You've got it all wrong.
MERCER (*rather annoyed*).   Really !   I don't see——
LOTTIE.   I think they want you to marry 'em.
MERCER (*glances astounded at the others*).   Marry them !
ANNIE (*rising, with spirit*).   'Ere, Maria, come on, do something.   (*To* MERCER.)   You'd better talk to Mr. Helliwell——

MARIA (*rising, takes his left arm*).   He's in the dining-room—just across——

(ANNIE *is now on his* L.   *They lead him out.*)

Ask him if he thinks you can do anything for us—(*now outside the room*) just in there—that's right——
CLARA (*crossing to* L. *of the chair* C.).   Which one was it ?

(LOTTIE *returns to her seat, smiling, as* MARIA *re-enters followed by* ANNIE, *who crosses to* R.C., MARIA *to* L. *of the bureau chair.*)

LOTTIE.   I think you missed a chance there—at least, two of you did.

(ANNIE *sits on the* R. *settee, lower end.*)

MARIA.   Two of us !   (*She takes the chair back to the bureau.*)
LOTTIE.   Well, you remember what I told you ?

(*She smiles reminiscently as* MARIA *comes down to the* L. *settee.*)

I'd known him here in Clecklewyke, but it was at Blackpool we really got going.   He said he was feeling lonely—and you know what men are, when they think they're feeling lonely—specially at Blackpool.
CLARA (*hastily*).   It couldn't have been Herbert.   He's never been to Blackpool without me.
ANNIE.   Yes, he has, Clara.   Don't you remember—about four years since—— ?
CLARA (*thunderstruck*).   And he said he hadn't a minute away from that Conference.   I'll never believe another word he says.   (*To* ANNIE, *coming to the head of the* L. *settee.*)   But your Albert was with him that time.
ANNIE (*grimly*).   I know he was.

(CLARA *sits on her* L.)

MARIA.   So was Joe.   (*She sits on the* L. *settee.*)   Said he needed a change.
LOTTIE (*sweetly*).   Well, we all like a change, don't we ?

(SOPPITT *enters up* L.C., *rather hesitantly.* CLARA *sees him first.*)

CLARA (*sharply, rising*).   Now, Herbert Soppitt——
SOPPITT.   Yes, Clara ?   (*He drops down a little.*)
LOTTIE.   Well, Herbert, how are you these days ?   (*Playfully.*)   You haven't forgotten me, have you ?
SOPPITT (L. *of* LOTTIE).   Forgotten you ?   I'm afraid there's a mistake——
CLARA (*grimly*).   Oh—there's a mistake all right.
MARIA.   Now, Clara, don't be too hard on him.   I expect it was only a bit o' fun.
SOPPITT.   What is all this ?

LOTTIE (*playfully*). Now, Herbert—— (*She rises.*)

SOPPITT (*indignantly*). Don't call me Herbert.

CLARA (*angrily*). No, wait till I'm out o' t'way.

ANNIE. I expect he didn't mean it.

SOPPITT (*annoyed*). Mean *what*?

(PARKER *now enters, rather wearily.* SOPPITT *turns to him.*)

I found that Mrs. Northrop, Albert. (*He turns away, crossing to below the* R. *settee.*)

LOTTIE (R. *of* PARKER). Oh—hello, Albert!

(CLARA *sits.*)

PARKER (*staring at her*). How d'you mean—*Hello, Albert?*

LOTTIE (*playfully*). Now, now—Albert!

(PARKER *crosses to* C., *looks at her in astonishment, then at the three women, finishing with his wife, who rises.*)

ANNIE (*bitterly, crossing to his* R.). Yes, you might well look at me, Albert Parker. You and your cheap holiday at Blackpool! I only hope you spent more on her than you've ever done on me.

PARKER (*vehemently*). Spent more on *her*? (*He steps up to her.*) I've never set eyes on her before. *Who is she?*

(LOTTIE *sits* C. ANNIE *and* CLARA *now look at each other, then at* MARIA, *who looks at them in growing consternation.*)

MARIA (*rising*). I don't believe it. I *won't* believe it.

(RUBY *looks in, excitedly.*)

RUBY. Mayor's motor-car stopping near t'front gate.

CLARA (*rises, shouting as* RUBY *goes*). Well, tell it to go away again. (*She sits.*)

(HELLIWELL *comes out of the dining-room, shutting the door, and begins speaking early. He bumps into* RUBY *in the doorway, as she exits.*)

HELLIWELL (*coming down* L.C., *flustered*). What with a photographer who's drunk, and a parson that's mad——! (*He sees* LOTTIE *now, and visibly wilts, and gasps.*) *Lottie!*

MARIA (*furiously*). Lottie!

CURTAIN.

ACT III

SCENE.—*The same, about a quarter of an hour later.*
RUBY *is tidying up the room, and also eating a large piece of
pasty. The camera is now stacked against the wall above the
conservatory doors.* RUBY *continues with her work several
moments after the rise of the* CURTAIN, *then* NANCY *makes cautious
appearance at the conservatory, sees that nobody but* RUBY *is
there, then turns to beckon in* GERALD, *and they both come into
the room.*

NANCY. What's been happening, Ruby ?
RUBY (*above the* R. *settee*). What 'asn't been 'appening ! Eee
—we've had some trade on wi' one thing an' another.
NANCY (*mischievous rather than reproachful*). You see what
you've done, Gerald.
RUBY. What ! He didn't start it, did he ? 'Cos if he did,
he's got summat to answer for. (*She crosses* C.)
NANCY (*crossing to her*, R.). Did—anybody ask where I was,
Ruby ?
RUBY (R. *of the* L. *settee*). No, an' I'll bet you could stop out
all night and they'd neither know nor care.
GERALD (*coming down in front of the* R. *settee*). But what *has*
been happening, Ruby ?
RUBY (*confidentially*). Place 'as been like a mad 'ouse this
last half-hour. To start with, Mayor o' Clecklewyke's been and
gone——
NANCY. The mayor ?
GERALD (*amused*). Why did they want to bring the mayor
into it ?
RUBY. Nobody brought him. He come of his own accord—
with a case o' fish-things an' wearing t'chain—like a chap in a
pantymime. He soon took his 'ook. But reporters didn't——
GERALD. Reporters, eh ?
RUBY. Ay, an' there were plenty of 'em an' all an' they didn't
want to go neither, not like t'mayor. So Mr. Helliwell an' Mr.
Parker took 'em into t'kitchen an' give 'em bottled ale an' for
all I know they may be there yet. Mrs. Helliwell's up in t'bed-
room—feeling poorly—an' Mrs. Soppitt's with her. Mr. Soppitt
an' Mrs. Parker's somewhere out in garden——
NANCY. I told you there was somebody there. (*She comes
down to* GERALD.)

RUBY. Ay, but let me finish. Now there's a woman wi' dyed 'air washing herself in t'bathroom upstairs—an' nobody knows what she wants—beyond a good wash. Down in t'dining-room there's a photographer who's right tiddly tryin' to argue with gert big parson—an' I'll bet he's makin' a rare mess—an' that'll be to do next.

(RUBY *exits.*)

GERALD. Sounds all very confused to me.

NANCY. Yes, and I'd better slip upstairs while nobody's about. Oh—Gerald. (*She goes up a little to* L.C.)

GERALD (*following her*). Nancy!

NANCY. Do you still love me?

GERALD. Yes, Nancy—still—even after a whole hour.

(*They kiss.* Enter SOPPITT *and* ANNIE *from the conservatory. They cross to* C.)

SOPPITT. Here, I say! You two seem very friendly!

ANNIE. I believe you were the girl he was seen with.

SOPPITT. Were you?

NANCY. Yes. We're practically engaged, you know. Only —I was frightened of saying anything yet to Uncle Joe.

SOPPITT. Well, don't start to-night——

ANNIE. Why shouldn't she? (*She sits* C.) He won't be quite so pleased with himself to-night as usual—just as I know another who won't.

NANCY. Good night.

ANNIE. Good night. Why don't you go outside and say good night properly. You're only young once.

(NANCY *and* GERALD *exit to the conservatory.*)

Yes, you're only young once, Herbert. D'you remember that time, just after you'd first come to Clecklewyke, when we all went on that choir trip to Barnard Castle?

SOPPITT. I do, Annie. As a matter of fact, I fancy I was a bit sweet on you then.

ANNIE. You fancy you were! I know you were, Herbert Soppitt. Don't you remember coming back in the wagonette?

SOPPITT. Ay!

ANNIE. Those were the days!

SOPPITT. Ay!

ANNIE. Is that all you can say—Ay!

SOPPITT. No. But I might say too much.

ANNIE. I think I'd risk it for once, if I were you. (*She rises, goes down* R.C.)

SOPPITT. And what does that mean, Annie? (*Following her.*)

ANNIE. Never you mind. But you haven't forgotten that wagonette, have you?

Soppitt. Of course I haven't.

(*He has his arm round her waist. Enter* Clara.)

Hello, Clara.

Clara. How long's this been going on ?

Annie. Now, don't be silly, Clara.

Clara. Oh—it's me that hasn't to be silly, is it ? I suppose standing there with my 'usband's arm round you bold as brass, that isn't being silly, is it ? I wonder what you call that sort of behaviour, then ?

Soppitt (R.C.). It was only a bit of fun.

Clara. Oh—an' how long have you been 'aving these bits o' fun—as you call them—Herbert Soppitt ?

Annie. You've a nasty mind, Clara.

Clara. Well—of all the cheek and impudence ! Telling me I've got a nasty mind. You must have been at it some time getting Herbert to carry on like that with you. Don't tell me he thought of it himself—I know him too well.

Annie. Oh—don't be so stupid, Clara. I'm going into the garden. I want some fresh air.

(*She goes out* R.)

Clara. Well, Herbert Soppitt, why don't you follow her and get some fresh air too ? Go on, don't mind me. Come here.

(*He doesn't move.*)

You 'eard me, come here.

Soppitt. Why should I ?

Clara. Because I tell you to.

Soppitt. I know. I heard you. But who do you think you are ?

Clara (*down to him*, C.). Herbert Soppitt—you must have gone wrong in your head.

Soppitt. No. Not me. I'm all right.

Clara (*sharply*). You'd better go home now, an' leave me to deal with this business here.

Soppitt (*bravely*). Certainly not.

Clara. In my opinion it's awkward with both of us here.

Soppitt. Well, *you* go home, then ? (*To below the* R. *settee.*)

Clara. What did you say ?

Soppitt (*bravely*). I said, *you* go home. You are doing no good here.

(*Very angry now she marches up to him and gives him a sharp slap on the cheek.*)

Clara. Now then ! (*She steps back and folds her arms.*) Just tell me to go home again !

Soppitt (*slowly, impressively, approaching her* C.). Clara, I always said that no matter what she did, I'd never lift a hand to my wife——

CLARA. I should think not indeed!

SOPPITT. But as you aren't my wife—what about this?

(*He gives her a sharp slap. She is astounded.*)

CLARA. Herbert!

SOPPITT (*commandingly*). Now sit down. (*He points to the* L. *settee.*)

(*She does not obey.*)

(*In a tremendous voice of command.*) *Sit down!*

(*She sits on the* L. *settee, staring at him. Then when she opens her mouth to speak.*)

Shut up! I want to think. (*He turns up stage.*)

(*A silence, during which she still stares at him. He stands* L. *of the* C. *chair.*)

CLARA (*in a low voice*). I don't know what's come over you, Herbert Soppitt.

SOPPITT (*fiercely*). You don't, eh?

CLARA (*gaping at him*). No, I don't.

SOPPITT (*severely*). Well, you don't think I put up with women coming shouting and bawling at me and smacking my face, do you?

CLARA. Well—you've never gone on like this before.

SOPPITT. Yes, but then before you were my wife——

CLARA (*hastily*). I'm your wife now.

SOPPITT. Oh no—you're not. (*He produces the letter.*)

CLARA. Give me that letter—— (*Half rising.*)

SOPPITT (*down a little* R.C.). Sit down—and shut up, woman!

(CLARA *sits. Enter* PARKER.)

PARKER. Where's Annie?

SOPPITT. She's out there somewhere—why don't you look for her?

CLARA. Perhaps she's hiding her face—and if you'd seen what I'd seen to-night, Albert Parker——

SOPPITT. Hold your tongue, before it gets you into mischief

CLARA. I'm only——

SOPPITT. Shut up.

PARKER. Here, but wait a minute—I'd like to hear a bit more about this—— (*To the* L. *of* SOPPITT.)

SOPPITT. Then you're going to be disappointed. (*To* CLARA.) You get back to Maria Helliwell, go on.

PARKER. Here, Clara, you're not going to——

SOPPITT. YOU mind you're own business. (*To* CLARA.) Go on—sharp.

(CLARA *rises, and exits up* L.C.)

PARKER. Herbert, 'ave you been 'aving a lot to drink ?

SOPPITT. I had a few, trying to find that Mrs. Northrop.

PARKER. I thought as much.

SOPPITT (*crossing to the front of the* L. *settee*). And I may possibly have some more, but whether I do or not, I'll please myself—just for once—and if any of you don't like it, you can lump it.

PARKER. Where did you say my wife was ?

SOPPITT. She's out there in the garden.

PARKER (*disapprovingly*). What—at this time o' night ? (*Looking towards the garden.*)

SOPPITT. Yes—and why not ?

PARKER (*with dignity*). I'll tell 'er that. I've no need to tell you. You're not my wife.

SOPPITT. No, and she isn't either. Don't forget that. (*He sits on the* L. *settee.*)

(PARKER *goes to the door and calls.*)

PARKER. Annie ! Hey—Annie !

SOPPITT. Why don't you go out and talk to her, instead o' calling her like that—as if she were a dog or something ?

PARKER. 'Cos standing about in damp grass this time o' night is bad for me. I don't want to start a running cold on top of all this. (*He calls again.*) Hey—Annie ! (*He returns to* R.C.) I came in to 'ave a few words in private with her——

SOPPITT. Oh—I'll leave you. (*Rising.*)

PARKER. In my opinion, there's been a lot too much talk among us altogether, too much noisy 'anky-panky, about this daft business. You might think we were a meeting o' t'gas committee way we've gone on so far. What's wanted is a few serious words i' private between us chaps an' our wives, an' less o' this public argy-bargy an' 'anky-panky.

(ANNIE *enters through the conservatory. She comes to below the* R. *settee.*)

Ah—so there y'are.

SOPPITT (*going up* L.C.). Well, best o' luck, Annie !

PARKER (*suspiciously*). How d'you mean ?

SOPPITT (*turning at the door*). Hanky-panky !

(*He goes out.* PARKER *goes up after him, then turns back.*)

PARKER. He's 'ad a drop too much, Herbert 'as ! Comes of running round the town after that charwoman.

ANNIE (*sits on the* R. *settee, amused*). Well, Albert ?

PARKER (*pompously and complacently now*). Well, Annie, I'm going to set your mind at rest. (*He comes a little down* L.C.)

ANNIE (*demurely*). Thank you, Albert.

PARKER (*as before*). Yes, I don't want you to be worrying. Now I think you'll admit I've always tried to do my duty as a 'usband.

ANNIE. Yes, Albert, I think you've always tried.

PARKER (*suspiciously*). What do you mean ?

ANNIE (*demurely*). Why—just what you mean, Albert.

PARKER (*after another suspicious glance, returns to the former tone, and is insufferably patronizing*). Of course, as nobody knows better than you, I'm in a different position altogether to what I was when I first married you——

ANNIE. When you *thought* you married me, Albert.

PARKER. Well, you know what I mean ! (*Down* L.) In them days, I was just plain young Albert Parker.

ANNIE. And now you're Councillor Albert Parker——

PARKER (*strutting up and down* L.C.). Well, an' that's something, isn't it ? And it isn't all, by a long chalk. I've got on i' business, made money, come to be a big man at chapel, vice-president o' t'Cricket League, on t'hospital committee, an' so forth—eh ? (*He finishes up* L.C.)

ANNIE. Yes, Albert, you've done very well.

PARKER (*complacently*). I know I 'ave. An' mind you, it's not altered me much. I'm not like some of 'em. No swank about me—no lah-di-dah—*I'm a plain man.* (*Down* C.)

ANNIE (*rather sadly*). Yes, Albert, you are.

PARKER (*looking at her suspiciously*). Well, what's wrong wi' it ? You're not going to tell me that at your time o' life——

ANNIE (*indignantly cutting in*). My time of life !

PARKER. Well, you're no chicken, are yer ? And I say, you're not going to tell me now, at your time o' life, you'd like a bit o' swank an' lah-di-dah !

ANNIE (*wistfully*). I've sometimes wondered——

PARKER (*brushing this aside*). Nay, nay, nay, nobody knows better than me what you'd like. (*Going* L.C., *he sits on the* L. *settee.*) An' you know very well what a good husband I've been —steady——

ANNIE (*rather grimly*). Yes, you've been steady all right, Albert.

PARKER (*complacently*). That's what I say. Steady. Reliable. Not silly wi' my money——

ANNIE (*same tone*). No, Albert, your worst enemy couldn't say you'd ever been silly with your money.

PARKER (*complacently*). And yet at the same time—not stingy. No, not stingy. Everything of the best—if it could be managed—everything of the best, within reason, y'know, within reason.

Annie. Yes, within reason.

Parker (*in a dreamy ecstasy of complacency*). Always reasonable—*and* reliable. But all the time, getting on, goin' up i' the world, never satisfied with what 'ud do for most men—no, steadily moving on an' on, up an' up—cashier, manager, share in the business—councillor this year, alderman next, perhaps mayor soon—that's how it's been an' that's how it will be. Y'know, Annie, I've sometimes thought that right at first you didn't realize just what you'd picked out o' t'lucky bag. Ay! (*He contemplates his own greatness, while she watches him coolly.*)

Annie (*after a pause*). Well, Albert, what's all this leading up to ?

Parker (*recalled to his argument*). Oh!—well, yer see, Annie, I was just saying that I thought I'd been a good husband to you. An', mind yer, I don't say you've been a bad wife—no, I don't——

Annie (*drily*). Thank you, Albert.

Parker (*with immense patronage, rises, crosses to her*). So I thought I'd just set your mind at rest. Now don't you worry about this wedding business. If there's been a slip up—well, there's been a slip up. But I'll see you're all right, Annie. I'll see it's fixed up quietly, an' then we'll go an' get married again—properly. (*Standing above her, he pats her on the shoulder.*) I know my duty as well as t'next man—an' I'll see that you're properly married to me.

Annie. Thank you, Albert.

Parker. That's all right, Annie, that's all right. I don't say every man 'ud see it as I do—but—never mind—I know what my duty is. (*He crosses back to down* L.)

Annie. And what about me ?

Parker (*puzzled, turning on her*). Well, I'm telling yer—you'll be all right.

Annie. How d'you know I will ?

Parker (*hastily*). Now don't be silly, Annie. (*Going up stage.*) If I say you'll be all right, you ought to know by this time yer *will* be all right. (*He selects a cigar from the box on the buffet.*)

Annie (*slowly*). But I don't think I want to be married to you.

Parker (*staggered*). What! (*He turns down sharply.*)

Annie (*slowly*). You see, Albert, after twenty-five years of it, perhaps I've had enough.

Parker (*horrified*). 'Ad enough! (*He comes down* C.)

Annie. Yes, had enough. You talk about your duty. Well, for twenty-five years I've done my duty. I've washed and cooked and cleaned and mended for you. I've pinched and scrimped and saved for you. I've listened for hours and hours and hours to all your dreary talk. I've never had any thanks for it. I've hardly ever had any fun. But I thought I was your wife and I'd taken you for better or worse, and that I ought to put up with you——

PARKER (*staring, amazed*). Put up with me!

ANNIE (*coolly*). Yes, put up with you.

PARKER. But what's wrong with me? (*He takes a step down.*)

ANNIE (*coolly*). Well, to begin with, you're very selfish. But then I suppose most men are. You're idiotically conceited. But again, so are most men. But a lot of men at least are generous. And you're very stingy. And some men are amusing. But—except when you're being pompous and showing off—you're not at all amusing. You're just very dull and dreary——

PARKER. Never!

ANNIE (*firmly*). Yes, Albert. *Very* dull and *very, very* dreary, and stingy.

PARKER (*staring at her as if seeing a strange woman*). 'As somebody put you up to this?

ANNIE. No, I've thought it for a long time.

PARKER. How long?

ANNIE. Nearly twenty-five years.

PARKER (*half dazed, half indignant*). Why—you—you—you little *serpent*!

ANNIE (*ignoring this*). So now I feel it's time I enjoyed myself a bit. I'd like to have *some* fun before I'm an old woman.

PARKER (*horrified*). Fun! Fun! What do you mean—fun?

ANNIE (*coolly*). Oh—nothing very shocking and terribly—just getting away from you, for instance——

PARKER (*in loud pained tone*). Stop it! (*He turns up stage.*) Just stop it now! (*He turns back.*) I think—Annie Parker—you ought to be ashamed of yourself.

ANNIE (*dreamily*). Well, I'm not. Bit of travel—and liveliness—and people that are amusing—and no wool business and town councillors and chapel deacons——

PARKER (*shouting angrily, crossing down to her*). Why don't you dye your hair and paint your face and go on t'stage and wear tights——

ANNIE (*wistfully*). I wish I could.

(*As* PARKER *groans in despair at this, crossing* L., RUBY *looks in.* PARKER *sits.*)

RUBY (*loudly and cheerfully*). Mr. Soppitt says if you haven't finished yet yer better 'urry up or go somewhere else to 'ave it out 'cos they're all coming in 'ere.

PARKER (*angrily*). Well, we 'aven't finished. (*He rises, goes up stage* R. *of* RUBY.)

ANNIE (*coolly*). Yes, we have.

(RUBY *nods and leaves the door open.*)

PARKER (*loudly, above chair* C.).   Now listen, Annie, let's just talk a bit o' sense for a minute——

ANNIE.   They'll all hear you—the door's open.

PARKER.   Nay—damn it——!   (*Up to the door.*)

(*He goes to shut the door but* SOPPITT *enters, followed by* CLARA.)

SOPPITT (*amused*).   Hello, Albert—what's made you look so flabbergasted.

PARKER (*annoyed*).   If I want to look flabbergasted, then I'll look flabbergasted, without asking your advice, Herbert.

SOPPITT.   Hanky-panky!   (*He comes down behind the* L. *settee.*)

PARKER.   Now shut up!   'Ere, Clara, yer wouldn't say I was stingy, would yer ?

CLARA.   Well, you've never been famous for getting your hand down, have you, Albert ?   (*Coming down in front of the* L. *settee.*)

PARKER (*indignantly*).   I've got my 'and down as well as t'next man.   I've always paid my whack, let me tell yer.   (*He sits on the chair* C.)   Call a chap stingy just because he doesn't make a big show—'cos he isn't—er——

ANNIE (*burlesquing his accent, coolly*).   Lah-di-dah !

SOPPITT.   Now stop tormenting him, Annie.

PARKER (*indignantly, rising, goes towards* SOPPITT.).   Tormenting me !   Nobody'll torment me.   And I like that coming from *you*, Herbert, when you've been a by-word for years.

CLARA (*angrily*).   A by-word for what ?

PARKER.   For years.

CLARA.   Yes, but a by-word for years for what ?

PARKER.   Oh !   Hen-pecked !   Ask anybody who wears the trousers in your house !

ANNIE.   Albert, don't be so vulgar !

PARKER (*to* R.C.).   Why, a minute since you wanted to wear tights.

ANNIE.   Only in a manner of speaking.

PARKER.   How can it be in a manner of speaking—'cos either you're wearing tights or you're not ?

(*Enter* LOTTIE, *and* HELLIWELL.)

LOTTIE.   What's this about tights ?

PARKER (*turning to her*).   Now you'll clear out right sharp—if you'll take my tip.   (*He goes up* C.)

LOTTIE.   And I'll bet it's the only kind of tip you do give too.   (*To* ANNIE.)   He looks stingy to me !   (*Coming a little down stage.*)

PARKER.   Stingy !   If anyone says that again to me to-night they'll get what for, and I don't care who it is.

(*He goes out up* L.C.)

HELLIWELL. For two pins I'd either leave this house myself
or else clear everybody else out. I've never seen such a place—
there's folk nattering in every damn' corner. (*He goes up stage.*)
ANNIE (*rises*). Where's poor Maria ?

(*She goes across towards the door.*)

SOPPITT. Clara !

(CLARA *exits after* ANNIE, SOPPITT *following.*)

HELLIWELL (*coming down a little*). Now, Lottie, be reasonable.
A bit o' devilment's all right, but I know you don't want to make
real mischief——

LOTTIE. Where's the mischief come in ? Didn't you say—
more than once—that if you hadn't been married already——
(*She moves a little* R.C.)

HELLIWELL (*urgently, coming down to her* L.). Now, you know
very well that were only a bit o' fun. When a chap's on a
'oliday in a place like Blackpool an' gets a few drinks inside 'im,
you know very well he says a lot o' damn' silly things he doesn't
mean——

LOTTIE (*indignantly*). Oh—I see. (*She sits.*) Just tellin' me
the tale an' then laughing at me behind my back, eh ?

HELLIWELL (*urgently, coming down to her* L.). No, I don't
mean that, Lottie. Nobody admires you more than I do.
You're a fine lass and a good sport. But you've got to be
reasonable. Coming 'ere *like this*, when you know as well as
I do, it were just a bit o' fun !

(MARIA *enters. She is dressed to go out, and is carrying some
housekeeping books, some keys, and several pairs of socks. These
can all be in a basket together.*)

MARIA (*grimly, a little below the door*). Just a minute, Joe
Helliwell !

HELLIWELL (*groaning*). Oh—Christmas ! (*Then sees she has
her outdoor things on.*) 'Ere, Maria, where are yer going ?

MARIA (*determined but rather tearful*). I'm going back to me
mother's.

HELLIWELL. *Your mother's !* Why, if you go to your mother
in this state o' mind at this time o' night, you'll give her a
stroke.

LOTTIE. That's right. She must be about ninety.

MARIA (*angrily*). She's seventy-two. (*She pauses.*) And
mind your own business. I've got some of it 'ere *for* you. (*She
comes down* L.C. *a little.*)

LOTTIE. What do you mean ?

MARIA (*indicating things she's carrying*). Some of your new
business, an' see 'ow you like it. You'll find it a change from
carrying on wi' men behind the bar.

HELLIWELL. What in the name o' thunder are you talking about ? (*She goes up* L.C. *and closes the door and returns.*)

MARIA. I'm talking about 'er. If she wants my job, she can 'ave it.

LOTTIE }(*together*). {(*Rising.*) 'Ere, just a minute——
                        {(*She crosses towards* MARIA.)
HELLIWELL}   {Now listen, Maria——

MARIA (*silencing them by holding up keys and rattling*). There's all t'keys, an' you'd better start knowing where they fit. (*She puts them on the table behind the settee.*) An' don't forget charwoman's just been sacked, an' I don't expect Ruby'll stay. You'll have to manage by yourself a bit. An' greengrocer calls at ten and the butcher calls at half-past——

HELLIWELL (*shouting*). What does it matter when t'butcher calls ?

MARIA (*calmly*). I'm talking to 'er, not to you. (*To* LOTTIE, *who looks astonished.*) These is the housekeeping books an' you'll 'ave to 'ave 'em straight by Friday or he'll make a rumpus. 'Ere you are.

LOTTIE (*backing away to* R.C.). I don't want 'em.

HELLIWELL (*harassed*). 'Course she doesn't——

MARIA. She can't run this house without 'em. You said so yourself. (*She throws the books on to the* L. *settee.*)

HELLIWELL. I know I did, but it's nowt to do with 'er.

MARIA. Then what did she come 'ere for ? (*To* LOTTIE, *producing the socks. She hangs them on the back of the settee.*) An' look, 'ere's five pairs of his socks and one pair of woollens that wants darning, and you'd better get *started* on 'em. An' upstairs you'll find three shirts and two more pairs of woollens you'll 'ave to do to-morrow, an' you'd better be thinking o' to-morrow's dinner 'cos he always wants something *hot* an' he's very *particular*—— (*She turns up towards the door.*)

LOTTIE (*aghast*). 'Ere, what do you think I am ?

HELLIWELL. Now, Maria, you're getting it all wrong. Nobody knows better than me what a good wife you've been. Now 'ave a bit of sense, love. It's all a mistake.

MARIA. And there's a lot of other things you'll have to manage, but while you're trying to manage them and him too, I'll be at Blackpool.

(*She exits, followed by* HELLIWELL.)

(*Enter* ORMONROYD.)

ORMONROYD. I know that face.

LOTTIE. Harry Ormonroyd.

ORMONROYD. Lottie, my beautiful Lottie. And you haven't forgotten me ?

LOTTIE. Forgotten you ! My word, if you're not off I'll saw your leg off. 'Ere, you weren't going to take their photos ?

ORMONROYD. Yes, group for "Yorkshire Argus." Make a nice picture—very nice picture.

LOTTIE. Nice picture! Don't you know? Haven't they told you? (*She roars with laughter.*)

ORMONROYD. Here now, stop it, stop it. Have a drink of port.

LOTTIE. Well, I suppose I might. (*She goes up to the buffet.*)

ORMONROYD (*pours out wine*). Certainly, certainly. Liberty 'All here to-night.

LOTTIE. Oh—it's Liberty Hall right enough. (*She takes the glass.*) Chin-chin.

ORMONROYD. All the best, Lottie. (*Down* C.)

LOTTIE (*on his* R.). Nice drop of port wine this. Joe Helliwell does himself very well here, doesn't he?

ORMONROYD. Oh yes, Lottie, you'll find everything very comfortable here. 'Ere, somebody told me you were back at the Talbot.

LOTTIE. I was up to Christmas. Who told you? Anybody I know?

ORMONROYD (*solemnly*). Yes—now just a minute. You know him. I know him. We both know him. I have him here on the tip of my tongue, but can't remember. Er—no. But I'll get him, Lottie, I'll get him.

LOTTIE. Then I had to go home. Our Violet—you remember our Violet—she married a sergeant in the Duke of Wellington's—the dirty Thirty-Thirds—and now she's in India.

ORMONROYD (*remembering, triumphantly*). Tommy Toothill!

LOTTIE. What about him?

ORMONROYD (*puzzled by this*). Nay, weren't you asking about 'im?

LOTTIE. No, I've something better to do than to ask about Tommy Toothill.

ORMONROYD (*still bewildered*). Quite so, Lottie. But what were we talking about him for? Didn't you say he'd gone to India?

LOTTIE. No, you fathead, that's our Violet. Oh—I remember, it must have been Tommy Toothill 'at told you I was working at the "Talbot"—d'you see?

ORMONROYD (*still bewildered*). Yes, I know it was. But what of it, Lottie? Aren't you a bit argumentative to-night, love?

LOTTIE (*good-naturedly*). No, I'm not, but you've had a couple too many.

ORMONROYD. Nay, I'm all right, love. 'Ere, what's happened to your Violet?

LOTTIE (*impatiently*). She married a sergeant and went to India.

ORMONROYD (*triumphantly*). Of course, she did. Somebody told me—just lately.

LOTTIE. I told you.

ORMONROYD (*reproachfully*). Yes, I know—I can 'ear. But so did somebody else. I know—Tommy Toothill!

LOTTIE. You've got him on the brain. Then at Whitsun—I took a job at Bridlington—but I only stuck it three weeks. No life at all—I told 'em, I says, " I don't mind work, but I do like a bit of life."

ORMONROYD. I'm just the same. Let's 'ave a bit of life, I say. An' 'ere we are, getting down in dumps, just because Tommy Toothill's gone to India.

LOTTIE. He hasn't, you piecan, that's our Violet. Nay, Harry, you're giving me the hump.

ORMONROYD. Well, play us a tune. Just for old time's sake.

LOTTIE (*going up to piano*). Aaaa, you silly old devil, I'm right glad to see you.

ORMONROYD (*follows her*). Good old times, Lottie, good old times.

(*They sing. They are interrupted by the entrance of* HELLIWELL, PARKER *and* SOPPITT.)

HELLIWELL. Now, what the hangment do you think this is—a tap-room ? " Yorkshire Argus " wants you on telephone.—

ORMONROYD. See you later.

HELLIWELL. And then get off home.

LOTTIE. Come on, love, I'll help you. (*She leads him off up* L.C.)

(*They exit.* PARKER *moves up* R.C., SOPPITT *to above the* L. *settee.* HELLIWELL L. *of the chair* C.)

PARKER. Now, what's wanted now is a few serious words in private together.

HELLIWELL. Yes, yes, Albert. I know. But give a chap time to have a breather. I've just had to persuade Maria not to go back to her mother's.

PARKER. Why, what can her mother do ?

HELLIWELL. Oh—don't start asking questions—just leave it, Albert, leave it, and let me have a breather. (*To the* R. *of* SOPPITT.)

(*Enter the three ladies, wearing their hats. They come to* C., ANNIE *is to the* R., *with* MARIA *in the* C., CLARA *to her* L.)

ANNIE. Now then, Albert—Joe—Herbert——

HELLIWELL. What is this, an ultimatum ?

MARIA. Joe Helliwell, I want you to answer one question.

HELLIWELL. Yes, Maria.

MARIA. Do you love me ?

HELLIWELL (*embarrassed*). Now, what sort of question is that to a chap—here ? Why didn't you ask me upstairs ?

MARIA (*solemnly*). Once and for all—do you or don't you ?
HELLIWELL. Yes, of course I do, love.
MARIA (*goes to the* L. *settee*). Then why didn't you say so
before ?

(CLARA *follows her.* ANNIE *crosses to the* R. *settee. All three
ladies sit, taking off their hats, putting them on the back of the
settees.*)

PARKER (*moving* C., *as if beginning to make a long speech*).
And now we're all by ourselves, it's about time we started to
put our thinking caps on 'cos we're not going to do any good
running round the 'ouse argy-bargying——
MARIA. That's right, Albert.
PARKER. Yes, but let me finish, Maria. We——

(*He is interrupted by* RUBY *appearing at the door.*)

RUBY. She's back !
MARIA. Who is ?
RUBY. That Mrs. Northrop. (*Withdraws, leaving door open.*)
HELLIWELL (*loudly, in despair, up to door*). Oh—Jerusalem—
we don't want 'er 'ere. . . .

(MRS. NORTHROP *appears, carrying bag, and flushed.* HELLIWELL
shuts the door.)

MRS. NORTHROP. If you don't want me 'ere, why did you
send 'im round chasing me and askin' to come back ? Yer
don't know yer own minds two minutes together. (*To* MARIA.)
You 'aven't settled up wi' me yet, y'know.
HELLIWELL (*annoyed*). Outside !
PARKER (*hastily, anxiously*). Half a minute, Joe, we can't
'ave her telling all she knows—— We'll be t'laughing stock o'
Clecklewyke to-morrow——
MRS. NORTHROP (*contemptuously*). Yer've bin that for years,
lad. I'd rather ha' Joe Helliwell nor you. Joe 'as 'ad a bit o'
fun in his time, but you've allus been too stingy.
PARKER (*the word again*). Stingy ! If anybody says that
again to me to-night, they'll get what-for an' I don't care who
it is.
HELLIWELL (*to* MRS. NORTHROP). I told you—outside—
sharp !
MRS. NORTHROP (*full of malice*). Suits me. I reckon naught
o' this for a party. You can't frame to enjoy yourselves. But
then there's one or two faces 'ere that 'ud stop a clock, never
mind a party. But wait till a few of 'em I know 'ears about it !
You'll 'ear 'em laughing at back o' t'mill right up 'ere.
PARKER. Now we can't let her go i' that state o' mind.
CLARA. You ought to charge 'er with stealin'.
MRS. NORTHROP (*horrified*). Stealin' ? Why—for two pins—

I'll knock yer lying 'ead off, missis. Never touched a thing i' my life that wasn't me own !

(RUBY *looks in, and* MRS. NORTHROP *sees her.*)

What is it, love ?

RUBY (*loudly, chiefly to* HELLIWELL). That photographer's asleep an' snoring bi telephone.

HELLIWELL (*irritably*). Well, waken him up an' tell him to go home.

(RUBY *withdraws.* MRS. NORTHROP *takes charge again.*)

MRS. NORTHROP (*significantly*). An' I *could* keep me mouth shut if it were worth me while——

CLARA (*almost hissing*). That's blackmail !

SOPPITT (*hastily*). Shut up, Clara !

MRS. NORTHROP (*looking at him*). Hello, *you've* come to life, 'ave yer ?

HELLIWELL (*to* MRS. NORTHROP). How much d'you want ?

MARIA (*angrily*). I wouldn't give her a penny.

CLARA (*quickly*). Nor me neither.

PARKER (*quickly*). Can we trust 'er—we've no guarantee.

SOPPITT (*quickly*). She could sign something.

ANNIE (*quickly*). That 'ud be silly.

MARIA (*quickly*). Not one single penny !

HELLIWELL (*angrily*). Will you just let *me* get a word in—an' be quiet a minute. Now then——

RUBY (*looking in*). Mr. Helliwell !

HELLIWELL (*impatiently*). What ?

RUBY. I wakened 'im an' told 'im to go 'ome. But 'e says 'e *is* at 'ome.

(*She withdraws as* HELLIWELL *bangs and stamps in fury up* C.)

HELLIWELL (*at top of his voice*). What *is* this—a bloody mad-'ouse ?

MERCER (*off, but approaching*). Mr. Helliwell ! Please !

HELLIWELL (*groaning*). Oh !—Jehoshaphat !—another of 'em ! (*He breaks to* L. *of* C.)

(MERCER *enters. He comes down on the* R. *of* HELLIWELL.)

MERCER (*sternly*). Mr. Helliwell, I cannot allow you to use such language. It's quite unnecessary.

HELLIWELL (*protesting*). You wouldn't think so if——

MERCER (*cutting in*). *Quite* unnecessary. A little patience—a little quiet consideration—that's all that is needed.

HELLIWELL. What—with folk like her ? (*Pointing to* MRS. NORTHROP.)

MERCER (*turns, surprised and disapproving*). Mrs. Northrop ! What are *you* doing here ?

MARIA (*quickly*). Making trouble !

MERCER (*before* MRS. NORTHROP *can speak*). Making trouble !
(*He stoops a little, near her.*) And you've been drinking again.

MRS. NORTHROP (*humble, crestfallen*). Only a drop or two—
just because I was a bit upset——

MERCER (*accusingly*). I'm ashamed of you, after all your
promises.

MRS. NORTHROP (*humble and flattering*). Oh—Mr. Mercer—
you're a wonderful man—an' you're t'only preacher i' Clecklewyke worth listening to. (*To the others, roundly.*) Aaaa !—
he's a fine preacher is Mr. Mercer. (*To* MERCER, *admiringly.*)
Like—like a—gurt lion of a man !

MERCER (*briskly, masterfully*). Now, Mrs. Northrop, flattery
won't help. You must make me a solemn promise.

MRS. NORTHROP (*looking up at him, humbly*). Yes, Mr. Mercer.

MERCER. Now promise me, solemnly, you will tell nobody
what you've heard here to-night. Now promise me.

MRS. NORTHROP (*in a solemn quavering tone*). I promise.
(*Making suitable gestures.*) Wet or dry . . . may I die.

MERCER. T-t-t-t-t. But I suppose that will do. Now off
you go, quietly home, and be a good woman. Good night, Mrs.
Northrop.

MRS. NORTHROP (*humbly*). Good night, Mr. Mercer, and thank
you very much. (*She turns at the door to address the company.*)
Aaaa !—he's a gurt lion of a man—— (*Fiercely, a parting shot.*)
Worth all you lot put together. (*She goes.*)

HELLIWELL (*with relief*). Well, we're rid o' one. (*To*
MERCER.) Now have you studied that letter, Mr. Mercer ?

MERCER (*producing it*). I've considered it very carefully.
(*Impressively.*) And you know what I think ?

SEVERAL OF THEM (*eagerly*). No ! Tell us ! (*Etc.*)

MERCER (*slowly*). This letter—in my opinion—is perfectly
genuine.

HELLIWELL (*disgustedly*). I thought you were going to tell
us summat we didn't know. (*Impatiently.*) Well—what the
hangment are we going to do, then ?

MERCER (*turning to him impressively*). My dear sir——
(*Then quickly.*) I don't know.

HELLIWELL (*disgusted*). Oh—Christmas !——

MERCER. But—if you want my final opinion, I think that if
there were less bad temper and bad language in this house, you
would have a better chance of settling your affairs.

HELLIWELL (*exasperated*). And *I* think I'm getting a bit tired
o' you, Mr. Mercer.

MERCER (*very angry, towering over* HELLIWELL). What !
After wasting my time, you now have the audacity—— Here——

(HELLIWELL *flinches, but it is the letter he is being given.*)

Good night, sir. Good night, ladies.

(*He marches out and bangs the doors.* HELLIWELL *breathes heavily and wipes his face, crossing to* L.C.)

HELLIWELL. Well, that's another we're rid of.

PARKER (*beginning in his usual style*). And now what's wanted——

CLARA (*cutting in, mimicking him*). What's wanted is a bit o' brainwork, and where we're going to get it from I don't know.

HELLIWELL (*behind the chair* C., *severely, to* CLARA). You'll get it from me if you'll keep quiet a minute.

(*A pause. They concentrate hard, and now* ORMONROYD, *still carrying a large glass of beer, comes in and sits down in the chair* C., *while they stare at him in amazement and disgust.*)

ORMONROYD (*cheerfully*). Now—let's see—what were we talking about ?

(HELLIWELL *breaks to* L. *of the chair* C.)

PARKER (*angrily*). We weren't talking about anything to you.

ORMONROYD (*ignoring this*). I wouldn't object to a nice hand at cards. (*To* HELLIWELL, *who is looking exasperated*). I like a game o' solo, don't you ?

HELLIWELL. No ! And I told you to get off 'ome.

ORMONROYD (*reproachfully*). Nay, but you want your photo o' t'group, don't you ?

PARKER. You'll take no photos 'ere to-night.

ORMONROYD. Now it's a funny thing you should ha' said that. I'm a chap 'at notices things—I 'ave to be in my profession—an' I've been telling meself there's people 'ere in this 'ouse to-night who isn't easy in their minds. No, there's summat a bit off 'ere—just you see. And people has to be easy in their minds to be photographed. (*To* HELLIWELL.) Nobody ever comes with the toothache, y'know, to 'ave their photos taken.

SOPPITT (*seriously*). No, I don't suppose they do. It never occurred to me—that.

ORMONROYD. Name, sir ?

SOPPITT. Soppitt.

ORMONROYD. Ormonroyd 'ere. There's thought in this face. I'd like to do it sometime in a nice sepia finish. Remind me, Mr. Soppitt.

(LOTTIE *enters.*)

Ah, there y'are, Lottie. (*He rises, to the* R. *of* LOTTIE.) Join the company.

MARIA (*to* LOTTIE, *rising*). I thought you'd gone long since.

HELLIWELL. You know very well you promised to go, half an hour since.

CLARA (*rises*). We ought to put police on you.

ANNIE. Clara !

ORMONROYD. Now what's the idea of picking on Lottie ? Why don't you live and let live. We're all in the same boat. We all come 'ere and we don't know why. We all go in our turn and we don't know where. If you are a bit better off, be thankful. An' if you don't get into trouble an' make a fool of yourself, well, be thankful for that, 'cos you easily might. What I say is this—— We're all human, aren't we ? (*Behind the chair* C.)

ANNIE. Yes, and thank you Mr. Ormonroyd.

PARKER. What yer thanking him for ? Who's he to start telling us what we ought to do ?

CLARA. Impudence, I call it.

(The telephone rings.)

ORMONROYD. Oh, me ? I'm nothing much. But in case you want to be nasty, Councillor Albert Parker, just remember though I may be nothing I 'appen to work for a newspaper. (*He comes a little down* C.) Behind me stands the Press, don't forget that, an' the Press is a mighty power in the land to-day——

(RUBY enters.)

RUBY. Telephone went and when I says " Who is it ? " chap said " Yorkshire Argus—is Ormonroyd, our photographer, there ? " an' when I says " Yes, he's still 'ere," he says " Well, tell him he's sacked." You're sacked. (*Sincerely.*) I'm sorry.

ORMONROYD. So am I, lass.

(RUBY exits. ORMONROYD looks around as if searching.)

I left a bag in 'ere somewhere. (*To down* R.)

LOTTIE. You must have left it down at " Lion," lad. (*She goes up to the buffet.*)

PARKER. I thought 'e couldn't carry corn. (*He breaks to the* R. *of* HELLIWELL.)

ANNIE. Shut up, Albert. (*She rises, goes to the* R. *of* PARKER.)

LOTTIE (*comes down to above the* R. *settee.*) Nay, Harry, you silly old devil, it's not so bad.

ORMONROYD (*turns back to* R.C.). It's not so good. (*He sits on the* R. *settee.*) Hard to know where to turn.

LOTTIE. Come on, lad, never say die. We've seen a bit of life an' we'll see some more before they throw us on the muck-heap. (*To the others.*) For two pins, I'd take him away now, and leave you to settle your own troubles—if you can.

HELLIWELL. Why—what's he got to do with our troubles ?

LOTTIE. Plenty. (*She sits above* ORMONROYD.) Now, Harry, tell 'em where you were married.

ORMONROYD. Nay, Lottie, they don't want to hear about my bad luck.
PARKER. We've enough of our own, without his.
ANNIE. No, Albert. Come on, Mr. Ormonroyd. (*Crossing to* R.C.)
LOTTIE. Tell 'em where you were married.
ORMONROYD. Lane End Chapel—five an' twenty years since.
HELLIWELL (*a step towards* PARKER). 'Ere, he must be in t'same boat with us, then!
ORMONROYD. Just another o' my bits of bad luck.

(ANNIE *sits* C.)

CLARA. We can understand that all right.
LOTTIE. Yes, but Harry 'ere had separated from his wife and they wanted to be free.
HELLIWELL. Well, what were they worrying for? They were free. Parson hadn't proper qualifications.
LOTTIE. Hold on a minute—go on, Harry.
ORMONROYD. I know he hadn't. Wife found that out. But what she'd forgotten, till I got a copy o' t'certificate is that in them days—twenty-five years since—chapel wedding—registrar had to be there an' all—to sign certificate.
PARKER. Joe, he's right.
ORMONROYD. I know damn' well I'm right. I've been carrying certificate for months trying to find a loophole in it—see for yourself.

(*He shows the certificate to* HELLIWELL, *who comes down, looks at it and returns to* PARKER.)

CLARA. Are we married after all?
HELLIWELL. Yes, of course we are. If parson didn't tie us up, registrar did—all legal—as right as ninepence.
CLARA. Aaaaa! Thank God!

(MARIA *crosses to the* L. *of* ANNIE, *who rises.*)

MARIA (*as she crosses*). Mr. Ormonroyd, this is best night's work you ever did. Thank you.

(ORMONROYD *and* LOTTIE *rise.*)

LOTTIE. Now then, Harry, buck up, lad. Why don't you take that little photo-shop in Blackpool again?

(CLARA *crosses to the* L. *of* MARIA.)

ORMONROYD. Nay, it 'ud cost me about a hundred pound to start it again—and I haven't a hundred shillings—an' I know you haven't.
LOTTIE. No, but there's folk here who'd never miss it.
PARKER. 'Ere, steady.

ANNIE. Albert, stingy again ?

PARKER. Nay, never—if that's how you feel—— (*Moving up to the* R. *of the desk.*)

HELLIWELL. We'll soon fix you up, Ormonroyd lad, leave it to me. (*Between* CLARA *and* MARIA.) By gow, you've taken a load off my mind—— Aaaaa—— Now then, everybody, let's brighten up. (*To door.*) Ruby . . . Ruby . . . bring some more drinks, lass. Owt you've got. Who'll give us a song ? ORMONROYD (*up to the piano*). Lottie's the one. Come on, Lottie, play us a tune.

(*They look through the sheet music.*)

CLARA (*crossing* L.C.). Now then, Herbert Soppitt, you see I am your wife after all. (*She sits on the* L. *settee.*)

SOPPITT. Yes, Clara, and I hope we'll be very happy. But we won't be if you don't drop that tone of voice. I don't like it. (*He sits above* CLARA.)

CLARA. No, Herbert.

SOPPITT. No !

PARKER (*rises to the* L. *of* HELLIWELL). 'Ere, Joe, you wouldn't say I was dull and dreary, would you ?

HELLIWELL. Ay, a bit, Albert.

PARKER. Well, that beats me. I've always seemed to myself an exciting sort of a chap. (*To* ANNIE, *coming down* R.C.) Anyhow, stingy or whatever I am, I'm still your husband.

ANNIE. So it looks as if I'll have to make the best of you.

MARIA. We'll all have to make the best of each other. But, then, perhaps it's what we're here for.

HELLIWELL (*at her side*). That's right, love.

PARKER. Well, we'd better see if we can have some of this fun of yours you talk about——

ANNIE. Aaaa—it doesn't matter, Albert.

PARKER. It does. I say we'll have some fun—— (*He sits above* ANNIE.)

(ORMONROYD *having found his camera by the conservatory door, brings it down* R.)

ORMONROYD. All in your places——!

(*They all take up " group positions," as he sets the camera up.*)

Now ! Steady—steady—everybody——

(*Enter* RUBY *with drinks. The flashlight goes off and she drops her tray.*)

CURTAIN.

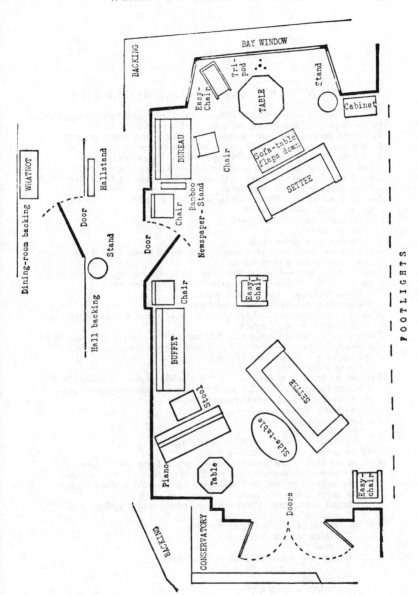

FURNITURE AND STAGE PROPERTIES

Stage.—Covered with green and brown Axminster carpet over stage cloth.
Down stage c.—Large polar bearskin with unmounted head.
Before the doors to the conservatory, R.—Small white sheepskin rug.
In the bay window L.—Red and blue Persian runner.
Before the door up stage c.—Turkey pattern Axminster rug.
Between the first and second backings up c.—Turkey carpet strip.
L.C.—Early Victorian 2-chair " spoon-back " settee in floral linen with
　　antimacassars and 3 cushions.
Behind above settee.—Square mahogany 3-foot table.
　On the table.—Velvet cloth.
　　Majolica vase with flowers.
　　Brass ashtray.
　　Leaf-shaped china dish.
R.C.—Bolster back and arm settee, 6 feet, in floral linen loose covers,
　　antimacassars and cushions.
Behind above settee.—Walnut Victorian table, shaped top, 3 foot 9 inches.
　On the table.—2 small silver and plush photo frames.
　　Brass ashtray.　Vase and flowers.
　　Cigar-box containing coloured counters.
Above the bearskin c.—Mahogany gent's easy chair in red velvet, with
　　antimacassar and cushion.
Down stage R., *below the doors.*—Mahogany Edwardian lady's easy chair.
Up stage R., *above the doors.*—Small mahogany octagonal table.
　On the table.—White lace D'oyley.
　　China female figure.
Up stage R., *to the* L. *of the above table.*—Upright piano, set obliquely, key-
　　board facing back wall.　Back of piano draped in green velvet.
　On the piano.—Red velvet runner.
　　Old sheet music.
　　Gold lustre jug.
　　Old photo frame.
　　WEDDING GROUP PHOTO (at downstage end).
L. *of the piano.*—Regency piano stool.
Against the back of the piano.—Folded green baize card table.
L. *of the piano* (*against the back wall*).—Mahogany-coloured buffet.
　On the buffet (*top shelf*).—2 alabaster and ormolu pagoda figures.
　　1 small china ornament.
　　Small rectangular silver tray, on edge leaning against wall.
　　1 small silver cup.
　(*Second shelf*).—White linen runner.
　　Tantalus with 3 decanters.
　　2 metal vases.
　　China match ball and Swan matches.
　　Box of ditto matches.
　　Brass ashtray.
　　Cigar-box with 6 cigars.
　(*Shelf in the under-part*).—2 small brass vases.
　　1 beaten brass plate.
　　1 ormolu fruit stand.

(*Bottom of the under-part*).—2 blue, white, and orange 7-inch china
    vases.
1 silver-plated Adams wine cooler.
R. *and* L. *of* C. *door.*—2 mahogany Edwardian chairs.
On L. *of* C. *door.*—A bamboo newspaper stand with periodicals.
To L. *of above.*—A mahogany Chippendale bureau.
On the bureau (*top shelf*).—2 Ramshead Ornaments.
    Silver photo frame.
    Silver calendar.
(*Pigeon-holes and flap*).—Stationery and playing-cards.
    Crochet work.
    Inkstand, and brass folding blotter.
    Bag with golden sovereigns.
Below the bureau.—Mahogany Edwardian chair.
Upstage corner of bay, L.—Victorian lady's easy chair, in floral linen, and
    antimacassar.
C. *of the bay* L.—Mahogany inlaid octagonal table.
    On the table.—Oriental vase.
    Green glass jug.
    Golden syrup tin with 6 peppermint creams in it.
    About 8 silver photo frames.
Between the above table and the window.—Bamboo tripod and aspidistra.
Downstage corner of the bay, L.—Black ebonized stand with brass jardiniere
    and fern in pot.
Downstage L., *below the bay.*—Sheraton cabinet.
    On the cabinet, L.—White lace D'oyley.
    Tall black and red vase.
Below the first backing up stage C. (R. *of door*).—Black ebonized stand as
    above, with aspidistra.
(L. *of the door*).—Black oak 2-foot hall-stand.
Against the second backing (*above the dining-room door*).—A walnut Vic-
    torian " what-not," with plated tea-urn and various china ornaments.
Curtains, conservatory doors.—Heavy red velvet.
    Bay windows.—Heavy green material.
    (Cornice poles and rings in mahogany.)
Wall pictures.—These are paintings, engravings, and prints of Edwardian
    and Victorian periods, such as :
    " Monarch of the Glen."
    " For Fifty Years." (*etc., etc.*)

LIGHTING PLOT

ACT I

Floats.—1 circuit frost $\frac{1}{2}$.
1 circuit 32 blue and frost *full.*
1 circuit 7 pink and frost $\frac{3}{4}$.
No. 1 *Batten.*—1 circuit white *full.*
1 circuit frost *full.*
1 circuit 32 blue and frost *full.*
1 circuit 7 pink and frost *full.*
No. 2 *Batten.*—2 circuits white *full.*
1 2,000 watt focus lamp (pink) through conservatory R.
2 1,000 watt floods 17 blue window L.
4 1,000 watt floods 17 blue conservatory R.

ACT II AND ACT III

Floats and battens as in ACT I.
All floods to 19 blue.
Chandelier, floor standard and 2 wall-brackets *alight.*

PROPERTY PLOT

ACT I

On the sideboard.—Cigar-box with 6 cigars. At the end of the Act, take three from Forbes and one from Helliwell.

Ashtray, match bowl, swan vestas.

On the piano.—Wedding group picture, and pile of music.

On the desk.—Bag with sovereigns.

On the table in the window.—Tin of sweets.

Off stage.—Letter and shilling for Forbes.

Camera case, black case, tripod for Ormonroyd.

Wet dish-cloth, drying cloth, meat dish for Mrs. Northrop.

Tray, 3 port bottles, 6 glasses for Ruby.

ACT II

Set card table c., in front of chair, with pack of cards and counters.

2 cigars back in box.

Port tray to the L. of sideboard, one cork out, 1 empty glass, 1 full glass.

Off stage.—String bag with parcels and two bottles for Mrs. Northrop.

Small purse for Mrs. Northrop.

Camera and black hood in case, lens and tripod with legs extended for Ormonroyd.

Tray with whisky decanter, syphon and 5 glasses for Helliwell.

ACT III

Strike camera case. Shorten legs of tripod and set camera with black hood upstage end of conservatory door.

Place flash tin and tripod on the table behind the R. settee.

Set cigar-box (1 cigar) to the R. of sideboard.

Set bun to the R. of sideboard.

Dust-pan and brush, c.

Off stage.—5 pairs of socks, pair of long pants, housekeeping books, bunch of keys for Maria.

2 pint glasses of brown ale, marriage certificate for Ormonroyd.

Tray with 3 bottles for Ruby.

MADE AND PRINTED IN GREAT BRITAIN BY
LATIMER TREND & COMPANY LTD PLYMOUTH

MADE IN ENGLAND